T0116468

Cambridge Elements ☰

Elements in Publishing and Book Culture
edited by
Samantha Rayner
University College London
Rebecca Lyons
University of Bristol

THE GENERAL READER AND THE ACADEMY

Medieval French Literature and Penguin Classics

Leah Tether
University of Bristol

CAMBRIDGE
UNIVERSITY PRESS

CAMBRIDGE
UNIVERSITY PRESS

University Printing House, Cambridge CB2 8BS, United Kingdom

One Liberty Plaza, 20th Floor, New York, NY 10006, USA

477 Williamstown Road, Port Melbourne, VIC 3207, Australia

314–321, 3rd Floor, Plot 3, Splendor Forum, Jasola District Centre, New Delhi – 110025, India

79 Anson Road, #06–04/06, Singapore 079906

Cambridge University Press is part of the University of Cambridge.

It furthers the University's mission by disseminating knowledge in the pursuit of education, learning, and research at the highest international levels of excellence.

www.cambridge.org
Information on this title: www.cambridge.org/9781108720175
DOI: 10.1017/9781108766715

© Leah Tether 2019

First published 2019

A catalogue record for this publication is available from the British Library.

ISBN 978-1-108-72017-5 Paperback
ISSN 2514-8524 (online)
ISSN 2514-8516 (print)

Cambridge Elements

The General Reader and the Academy

Medieval French Literature and Penguin Classics

Elements in Publishing and Book Culture

DOI: 10.1017/9781108766715

First published online: 2019

Leah Tether

University of Bristol

Author for correspondence: Leah Tether leah.tether@bristol.ac.uk

ABSTRACT: Penguin Classics have built their reputation as one of the largest and most successful modern imprints for 'classic' texts on the notion of 'the general reader'. Following an interrogation of this idea, Leah Tether investigates the publication of medieval French literature on this list and shines a light on the drivers, motivations, negotiations and decision-making processes behind it. Focusing on the medieval French texts published between *c.* 1956 and 2000, Tether demonstrates that, rather than Penguin's frequently cited 'general reader', a more academic market may have contributed to ensuring the success of these titles.

KEYWORDS: Penguin Classics, Medieval French, academy, general reader

ISBNs: 9781108720175 (PB), 9781108766715 (OC)

ISSNs: 2514-8524 (online), 2514-8516 (print)

Contents

1 Introduction: 'The Penguins are coming!'[1]

The story of Penguin Books is practically the stuff of legend. A flash of inspiration reportedly hit its founder, Allen Lane, at Exeter train station in 1932. Upon scouring the shelves of the station stall for something, anything, to read on his journey home to London, he realised that there was simply nothing of substance available. What if, he mused, quality literature were available for the price of a packet of cigarettes? And so 'Penguins', as they came affectionately to be known, were born (Penguin Books, 1985, pp. 13–15; Lewis, 2006, pp. 71–3; Rylance, 2005, p. 48). Of course, the full story is far more complicated than that, but the principle of the establishment of Penguin Books was simple: to make quality texts available at an affordable price, or 'GOOD BOOKS CHEAP', to borrow the phrase that Lane (1938a, p. 969) would later coin as his slogan. It would be a mistake, though, to view Allen Lane's 'eureka!' moment as one born purely out of an ideological desire to educate the masses, to make reading an affordable pastime for a wider demographic. Undoubtedly, as Lane's legacy would show, this may have formed some part of his thinking, but he was also a businessman, a seasoned publisher who understood from first-hand experience the changing book-market trends of the 1930s, which had led to a significant downturn in the fortunes of his existing company, The Bodley Head (De Bellaigue, 2001a, p. 70). The problem was that reading itself was not what needed encouragement, rather the actual purchasing of books.

After the First World War, thanks in large part to the institution of compulsory primary schooling from the 1880s onwards, more sophisticated levels of literacy were becoming increasingly widespread, and so a demand for evermore reading materials inevitably followed. However, the sheer price of new books meant that access was still problematic. Consequently, the reading public often shunned the bookshop, instead using public libraries, second-hand books and books borrowed from friends. Added to this, books tend not to 'wear out' and require replacement, as do other

[1] This was the shout line appended to the advertisement for a set of ten new Penguins that Allen Lane placed in the 1935 issue of The Bodley Head's journal, *Bodleian*. This advertisement is reproduced in Penguin Books (1985, p. 17).

commodities,[2] and so the publisher was, and is, faced with a significant challenge (Rylance, 2005, pp. 48–50). This challenge was less to engage the public with reading for pleasure than to compel them to acquire books as personal property. In some ways, and with the glorious benefit of hindsight, the answer should have been obvious, but many publishers of considerable standing nonetheless found themselves on their uppers. Twenty-one major firms, including Lane's own Bodley Head, went out of business in the 1930s (Rylance, 2005, p. 49). Even when confronted with Lane's idea to harness the paperback form,[3] the notion induced a deep suspicion amongst publishers, critics and authors – a fear that overproduction would drive down standards and that short-term gain would lead to long-term cultural detriment (Lewis, 2006, pp. 70–1). George Orwell, for instance, was outspoken in his belief that people's book-buying habits were finite due to how much reading time a single person had. He predicted the publishing trade's imminent collapse in the face of the Penguins' market infiltration: 'the cheaper books become, the less money is spent on books. This is an advantage from the reader's point of view and doesn't hurt trade as a whole, but for the publisher, the compositor, the author and the bookseller it is a disaster' (Orwell, 1936, p. 165). How wrong Orwell would be. And he was far from alone. Other notable publishers of the time pleaded with Lane to see sense,

---

[2] Simon Eliot (2013, p. 2) actually cites the 'reassuring flimsiness' of the Penguin paperback as one of its key selling points, but even these more-fragile-than-usual books remain amongst the most durable items of personal property, as evidenced by their still adorning bookshelves the world over: thumbed, broken spined and falling apart, they are still – more or less – readable.

[3] The 'invention' of the paperback is popularly attributed, incorrectly, to Lane; in fact, the paperback existed at least as early as the nineteenth century, and some even date it to the Aldus Manutius's sixteenth-century Aldine Press (Lewis, 2006, p. 75; Lamb, 1952, p. 39), but it was usually the format employed for low-brow, popular novels and thus associated with works of inferior quality, often called 'yellowbacks' after their mustard-coloured paper covers (Raven, 2014, pp. 151–2). Alastair McCleery (2002, pp. 164–9) provides a particularly pragmatic account of Lane's inspiration and its subsequent effect on the trade, which is helpfully devoid of sentiment.

such as the managing director of Chatto and Windus, Harold Raymond, who in a letter to Lane wrote the following:

> The steady cheapening of books is in my opinion a great danger in the trade at present, and I sometimes think booksellers have to be saved from themselves in this respect. . . . [I]t is this lowering of prices which is one of the chief reasons why our trade is finding it so hard to recover from the slump.
> (Raymond to Lane, 1 November 1934, quoted in Penguin Books, 1985, p. 15)

Even after Penguins had started paying dividends, Lane's contemporaries continued to ascribe the trade's various woes to them: 'You're the b . . . that has ruined this trade with your ruddy Penguins', was the insult reportedly levied at Lane by Jonathan Cape, who was undoubtedly frustrated at his own lack of vision. Cape had, after all, been the first publisher to lease the rights to several key titles that would launch Penguin, mistakenly assuming that the initiative would not go anywhere and that he might as well make a profit out of Lane before it all went wrong (Howard, 1971, p. 164). In the end, these and other publishers' long-held perceptions of what constituted the restrictions on intelligent reading, which were also those that underpinned the core assumptions governing the publishing trade's commercial practice, would turn out to be misplaced (Rylance, 2005, p. 53). Lane's decidedly contrary view, arguably more a product of luck than judgement, was that the only restriction on intelligent reading was personal purchasing power. This transpired to be the luckiest of hunches.

The aim of this Element, however, is not to trace a potted history of the founding of Penguin Books – a task undertaken many times already (see, for example, Eliot, 2018; Penguin Books, 1960, 1985; Williams, 1956). This said, the gap in the market that Lane astutely identified, and thus the basis upon which the resulting 'paperback revolution' was instigated, claims an importance for the enquiry that follows. Even if Lane's motivations were fundamentally economic, the trigger for finding the answer to the trade's issue was his realisation that good quality literature needed to be more widely available. His solution would involve, in short, not only targeting but also cornering a wider demographic than the trade had hitherto attempted. Lane would need to bring good books to the masses (Hare, 1995, p. xii). The upshot of this scheme was a manifest fixation of Lane's business on creating products that would appeal to a somewhat mysterious character, one who is, however, referred to with remarkable frequency in both the myriad correspondence in the Penguin Archive[4] and the published scholarship on Penguin's business that together underpin this Element. This elusive character goes by the moniker of 'the general reader'.

Nowhere do we hear more of our general reader than in relation to the book series that perhaps most keenly embodies the Penguin brand: Penguin Classics. Foreshadowed to some degree by Penguin's issue of six Shakespeare plays in 1937 (Morpurgo, 1979, p. 113), the founding of the Classics in 1944 (first publication 1946) under the leadership of E. V. Rieu (who served both as the series' editor and as the translator of its inaugural publication, Homer's *The Odyssey*) was not dissimilar from the initial establishment of Penguin Books. Despite widespread commercial advice that the idea of bringing 'classic' texts to the masses would have no traction in the marketplace, Lane nonetheless backed it. He may have been driven in this endeavour by prevalent contemporary domestic concerns in respect of the conditions to which British people would return from the Second World War, as adumbrated in the liberal economist William Beveridge's report published in November 1942,[5] which outlined plans for tackling the 'Five Giant Evils' of Society (Want, Disease, Ignorance, Squalor and Idleness), and which may have become the blueprint for Labour's welfare state in 1945 (Whiteside, 2014, p. 24).[6] Probably not unrelated was the fundamental belief that the new

[4] The Penguin Archive is housed today in Special Collections in the University of Bristol's Arts and Social Sciences Library.

[5] The report was officially titled: 'Social Insurance and Allied Services (Cmd. 6404)' (Beveridge, 1942).

[6] The Beveridge Report, in turn, was a product of discussions that came as a result of the poor conditions to which soldiers returned (poor housing provision and healthcare) after the First World War, and the desire to avoid the same happening a second time. For more on this topic, see Harris (1997, chs. 16–18).

'citizen soldier' of the Second World War needed to be educated (in contrast to his more accepting forefathers in the First World War), so that he could understand the reasons for fighting in the war. Significant investments of time and money were thus made into the Army Bureau of Current Affairs (ABCA), which conducted weekly reading groups for the millions working in the armed forces on issues relating to citizenship but also history, geography and religion (Huxford, 2018, pp. 16–17, 77–8; Grant, 2016).[7] Such factors surely influenced Lane's strategy, and he was richly rewarded for his investment of faith. Lane's ambition to distance 'classic' texts from their traditionally academic associations ('to break away from the academic idiom' as Penguin Editor Bill Williams (1956, p. 19) would later describe Rieu's mantra for the Classics) and make them accessible to larger audiences was a runaway success. *The Odyssey*, which sold more than three million copies, became the bestselling Penguin of all (Yates, 2006, p. 35; Shorley and McCann, 1985, p. 9).

It is in this very context of 'unlikely candidates for publishing success' that I situate the Element that follows. If Homer was considered to have had dubious potential as a bestselling author, even in spite of the likelihood that a reading public would have at least heard tell of his works (and those of other celebrated authors writing in Greek and Latin, upon whose corpus of writings Penguin Classics had initially been founded (Lewis, 2006, p. 252)), at what point – and why – did Penguin Classics believe the time was ripe to mine the works of other, more obscure authors? And was the process of bringing them to market really as distanced from the academy as Penguin's 'self-understanding', to use William John Lyons's (2013, p. 69) term, would have us think?

To explore these questions, the subject of my interest here is the move from *c.* 1956 until the turn of the millennium towards medieval literary authors. Of course, it takes little imagination to understand why a narrative such as Sir Thomas Malory's *Le Morte Darthur*, and indeed

[7] ABCA would stop in the 1950s, but the notion of needing well-read citizens continued, even becoming more important, throughout the Cold War, with the notion of being well informed constituting a defining principle of democracy over communism (Huxford, 2018, pp. 77–8).

other medieval works in the English vernacular, came quickly to be added to the Penguin Classics list – though even these 'safe bet' endeavours were not without their own complications.[8] But what of the translation of medieval literary works from other European vernaculars, whose authors were largely unknown to an anglophone reading public? On what basis would they be saleable? In a trade which is notoriously risk averse, the various hunches of Lane notwithstanding, why would this risk be worth it? This concise Element will trace the route to market of Penguin's medieval French literary works, asking whether our friend, the general reader, really can have been the intended target market. I have elected to focus on Penguin's medieval French titles, first, for pragmatic reasons – the extent of the corpus, composed of eleven titles, is ideal for a study of this length and remit. Second, and more important, from my perspective as an academic working in medieval French, the texts selected for Penguin's medieval French Classics have come to form the core of undergraduate curricula in medieval French (and often English) in both the United Kingdom and the United States, which raises important questions in respect of Penguin's influence and 'canonisation' (a term to which I will return). Third, I believe that the French list highlights some core differences in the way Penguin approached translations from languages other than Old/Middle English, Latin and Greek. The Element is thus split into two sections. The first of these takes a macro view of the identity of the general reader, and Penguin's attempts to reach them, as well as of how 'classics' (and indeed Penguin Classics) may have come to be inextricably linked with the academy. This provides the context for the second section, which homes in on the archival evidence surrounding Penguin's publication of medieval French literary titles, where I conduct an enquiry into whether the realities adumbrated by the Penguin Archive's primary evidence actually fit with the broader horizon in which Penguin was, and purported to be, operating. There is, of course, still much work to be done on the sociocultural conditions governing the publishing trade in post-war Britain; whilst this

[8] See the forthcoming Element in Publishing and Book Culture by Samantha J. Rayner on this subject. Rayner (2018) has also discussed the subject in a recent article on what she calls 'The Ship-Wrecked Malory'.

Element does not aim to give a full overview of these conditions, its case study–based approach nonetheless offers an insight into how Penguin chose (and was forced) to operate during that period, particularly in respect of translating foreign-language works. Therefore, in addition to furnishing information as to Penguin's internal commercial concerns in respect of Classics, it also provides some initial redress to the gap in our understanding of the sociology of knowledge, influenced by the rise of intellectual culture and changing class relations, in post-war Britain.

2 The General Reader, the Academy and Penguin Classics

2.1 Who Is the 'General Reader'?

I referred to the general reader in my introduction as an elusive character, and yet the concept has become such a commonplace, a kind of stock phrase, that I think most would probably have an initial sense of to what/ whom this refers. Such an individual might just as easily be referred to as an 'average joe/jane' or 'the (wo)man in the street', but does this really tell us anything about her or him? Indeed, for a term that is used so frequently and with such abandon, actually defining what is meant by 'the general reader' turns out to be a more complex affair than it at first seems. Taking the perspective of the publisher: how can these readers be attracted to book products if the publisher knows nothing other than that she or he is average? What does that really mean, in specifics? After all, it is upon specifics that the principles of marketing are founded. The successful strategic creation of a book product rests upon the identification of a circumscribed target market, and the sketching of a figure for whom the product is meticulously tailored and at whom associated campaigns are aimed (Squires, 2007, p. 51). Indeed, in her brief blog reflection on leading an MA Publishing class on book proposals at Oxford Brookes University, Alison Jones (2016) argues strongly that designating books as intended for general readers is 'lazy', not only because it is impossible to reach such an ill-defined market but also because it implies that a publisher has not thought deeply enough about that market. This in turn risks alienating rather than attracting readers, precisely because readers do not think of themselves as general, but rather as individuals with their own unique experiences and preferences.

Even if we imagined for a moment that parameters could be agreed for what constitutes 'general' or 'average', given the fairly vast spectrum that would have to be acknowledged, how can Lane, and Penguin by association, possibly have hoped to appeal to this wide a demographic? Lane's was by no means a 'lazy' enterprise, to return to Jones's term, but it was one founded more upon instincts than proven stratagem. We might legitimately ask, then, did Penguin and Lane even know what they meant by 'the general reader'? Did they mean it to refer to something or someone specific, understood internally if not externally, or was it merely a useful placeholder term, designed simply to give the impression that Penguin knew what it was doing? If the former, then what, exactly? And, if the latter, did the books find their way accidentally to a target market that was rather more specific than the general reader designator would have us believe? As Jones (2016) puts it so succinctly, to say a book is for the general reader is no better than saying '"[t]his book is for humans". Well, yes, but that's not very helpful, is it?' Indeed not, so I will now explore this more deeply.

What we can be assured of is that the general reader was by no means Lane's invention, nor was it peculiar to Penguin Books. The term was already in wide use amongst book professionals well before the time of Lane's epiphany on Exeter station, as is evidenced, in just one of several examples, by the 1931 appearance of a scholarly article in a librarianship journal (Waples, 1931). In it, the author Douglas Waples grapples with the librarian's age-old problem of choosing which books to buy for his library because, he says, 'almost everybody reads different amounts of everything for all sorts of reasons', a statement he describes as 'hopelessly vague' (Waples, 1931, p. 190). Waples thus undertakes a quantitative analysis of the relative popularity of given genres of books to see if he can apply a general rule to the proportion of books in particular genres that it would be sensible to purchase. Following this through to its logical conclusion, therefore, whilst Waples' general reader sounds like she or he is a single person who embodies everything in an average way, in fact Waples is talking about 'readers plural', and what constitutes the perfectly literal average of their reading habits. In short, there is no general reader in

Waples' model: there are lots of readers, and his attempt is to find a way to cater to them all, not with one single item but with a range of items that ensures that there is something for everyone.

This conception of the general reader as, in fact, 'readers plural' is somewhat easier to grasp than the notion that one item could please all, and it makes a good deal of sense, but it leaves open the fundamental problem that Penguin's usage of it appears to speak to something rather different. Indeed, Penguin's mode of operating was not, in the manner of Waples' library purchases, to build a list, the sum total of which would mean that everyone could find something they liked, but rather that each individual item on the list had been chosen for its potential to appeal to the still undefined general reader – what we now recognise as Jones's 'lazy' route to market. So the question remains as to whether Penguin really had a sense of to whom it was marketing its books. Lane may have been an occasional risk-taker, but it would be too much of a stretch, surely, to paint him as someone who really thought it was possible to please everyone with every single product.

What *would* make sense is less the idea that Lane wanted to create products for *everyone*, but rather products that at least held the potential to be used by *anyone*, as is suggested by Morpurgo's (1979, p. 215) slightly insensitive albeit accurate description of Lane's business strategy as being akin to 'blanket-bombing'. Still, though, it remains to be seen whether we can discover who 'anyone' actually was or is. Anecdotally, of course, very few readers, at least in anglophone countries, could claim never to have encountered a Penguin Book. But, as Eliot (2013, p. 1) advocates in his prehistory of Penguin, 'all book history should begin and end with a reader. Not a generalised reader, not a convenient reader devised by a literary critic, but with a real reader at a precise time.' Fortunately for us, there are various 'real' Penguin readers who have taken the trouble to record their experiences and engagements with Penguins, and their insights may help us to grasp better who actually ended up reading Penguins, and why.

Richard Hoggart (1960), writing on the occasion of Penguin's Silver Jubilee, offers his thoughts in a short piece in *Penguins Progress* entitled 'The Reader'. When Penguins first came to market, Hoggart recalls that he was sixteen and a 'working class youth at a grammar-school'. Despite acknowledging that he does not believe that anyone can claim to be a typical reader, he somewhat contradicts himself by saying he believed himself to have been 'roughly typical of one large group of Penguin's early customers' (p. 27). Hoggart states, perhaps unsurprisingly, that cheapness was a factor in his generation's enthusiasm towards Penguins; he interestingly adds that success may have had more to do with a timeliness that was predicated upon the post-war rise in intellectual activity amongst a larger social demographic than ever before.[9] This meant that Hoggart and his friends felt a need 'to keep up with the Joneses, culturally and intellectually'. For Hoggart, what Penguin got so right was finding a balance: the books were accessible without being dumbed down; they were aspirational, but not beyond reach (pp. 28–9). Hoggart also acknowledges that as he matured, so did his relationship with Penguins, coming as he did to view them not just through a reader's eyes but additionally through those of a teacher and later of a parent (p. 29). In all of these interactions, though, what is clear is that Hoggart is not thinking as just 'anyone'. He is unambiguous in proclaiming Penguins as holding an appeal specifically for intellectually and culturally engaged readers: Hoggart himself went into the academic profession, rising to be a professor of English, and Warden of Goldsmiths, University of London, and he even ends his short reflection by noting that his own Penguin Book had prompted letters from 'readers who are clearly laymen and young, but whose seriousness and critical intelligence is [*sic*] certainly no less than we [Hoggart and his peers] could claim'. In Hoggart's depiction, then, the general reader turns out to be a long way from 'general', instead finding a rather more precise definition bounded by intellectual culture.

Twenty-five years later, Penguin Books (1985) published a further celebratory volume to mark its fiftieth anniversary. Another self-professed Penguin reader and English professor would provide the foreword: Sir Malcolm Bradbury. Bradbury (1985, p. 8) reflects on his experience of Penguins as follows:

---

[9] Particularly useful studies of the radically changing sociocultural conditions that affected the publishing trade in the post-war period are provided by Rose (2001, esp. ch. 4) and Collini (2012; 2008, esp. ch. 21).

> When I was an avid youthful reader, the Penguin book
> became the basis of my literary education. I read *Penguin
> New Writing* with voracity, and celebrated when ten Evelyn
> Waughs and ten D. H. Lawrences came out together. When
> I was a student, at the start of the 1950s, there was still
> a curious impropriety about accumulating a library largely
> made up of paperbacks, but I was able in this way to build up
> a collection of personal classics in all the major areas, from
> the fiction of the past and present, through poetry and drama
> to philosophy and history. This was, for me, the importance
> of the paperback revolution: the endless extension of the
> canon of reading. I came to regard Penguin Books, not as
> a publishing house, but as a major national institution, like
> the BBC, and noted whom it honoured, and whom it failed
> to honour.

Whilst Bradbury's reminiscences say less about the ability of Penguins to improve social status through offering the means by which to become widely read without breaking the bank, this account is, in some ways at least, not dissimilar from that of Hoggart. Even though Bradbury actually seems to regard having Penguins on your shelf as being close to the opposite of having a set of status objects (perhaps less a tool for keeping up with the Joneses than Hoggart would have us believe), his unapologetic positioning of Penguins as net contributors to his education speaks very much to Hoggart's view of things. And this should perhaps not surprise us, for both Bradbury's and Hoggart's subsequent careers in the academy, specifically in literary study, are not unalike.

Completing a trio of published critical reflections on being a Penguin reader is the rather more recent article by David Cannadine (2013). Included in the edited volume released to herald the completion of the Arts and Humanities Research Council–funded Penguin Archive Project which ran from 2008 to 2012,[10] Cannadine's piece offers a critical reflection

[10] The project website remains accessible, at the time of writing, at www.bristol.ac.uk/penguinarchiveproject. A more permanent and detailed

on his changing relationship with Penguins over the course of his life. Of the three, Cannadine's is in some ways the most self-aware. He attempts to strike a careful balance between offering a personal think piece and a critical study that demonstrates an understanding of the complex issues involved in defining a publisher's intended audience, particularly retrospectively. Cannadine acknowledges the same issue as does Eliot in respect of book history's need to start with a precise reader and thus sets himself up in that role. In his words:

> This essay seeks to circumvent these problems by describing the relationship between a precisely defined reader and a well-documented publisher over a short but significant span of time. The precisely defined reader is myself, the well-documented publisher is Penguin Books, and the short but significant span of time was the ten years of my life from the late 1950s (when I was at primary school) to the end of 1968 (when I left grammar school *en route* to Cambridge). (p. 92)

Although Cannadine acknowledges that his personal reflections may not be complete or even accurate, he justifies the choice of himself thus: 'I suspect that my reading experiences during these years were widely shared by many members of the Welfare State generation to which I was lucky enough to belong' (p. 92). In other words, like Hoggart, Cannadine believes himself to have been another 'typical' Penguin reader, a person apparently created by the eleven-plus grammar/comprehensive secondary schooling system, for which the foundations were laid by the 1944 Education Act (or Butler Act), one of the most important and earliest pieces of legislation to enact William Beveridge's vision for tackling 'ignorance' (Simon, 1991, pp. 65–72). Indeed, and again similar to Hoggart and Bradbury before him, Cannadine spends a considerable part of his pseudo-memoir in describing how closely linked were his

summary of the project's aims and objectives is provided in the preface to the edited volume itself (Wootten and Donaldson, 2013, pp. xiv–xv).

engagement with Penguins and his education – Penguins were, in his words, an 'unrivalled route to knowledge and learning and information' (p. 98). Once again, then, we have a young man from the aspirational classes who used Penguin Books as sources of learning, both informally in his spare time, and formally in the classroom and lecture hall where Penguins were often prescribed set texts. Cannadine would also eventually become a professor, albeit of history rather than English. These three Penguin readers, therefore, are actually rather alike and thus represent precisely the inverse of 'general'. Whilst, of course, there is no denying that the sorts of readers likely to publish reflections on their reading habits are always going to be 'of a type', we could be forgiven for thinking – on this evidence at least – that the actual audience for Penguins came from a fairly narrow demographic, and probably even one that is quite explicitly gendered.[11]

Indeed, for all the talk of the general reader, occasional statements by the early Penguin protagonists do tend to betray that the general reader may have been rather more consciously specific than both the designation and the usual accompanying puff suggest. Lane (1938b, p. 42) himself, for instance, lambasted his fellow publishers in a piece in the *Penrose Annual* by saying that the days had long since passed of 'the publisher who imagines that the majority of people are stupid, interested only in entertainment that enables them to escape from their environment'. Here, he acknowledges the broadening intellectual culture in which his business was operating, although at this point he appears to ascribe intellectual curiosity to the realms of a majority of readers: perhaps, therefore, Lane had an extremely generous view of the general reader and her or his intellectual capacity? Elsewhere, though, Lane's turns of phrase appear to suggest that his view of

---

[11] This is a point also confirmed in Richard Hornsey's (2018, pp. 814–15) study, based on research conducted by Penguin itself in 1947. There is not space here to do justice to a discussion of gender and the general reader and, though I will allude to it again later, the subject will be discussed in more detail in a forthcoming Element in Publishing and Book Culture by Rebecca E. Lyons. Additionally, more information on the experience of the grammar school girl in the post-war period and how it differed from that of the likes of Hoggart and Cannadine is provided by Walkerdine (1997) and Steedman (1986).

the reading public was actually rather more segmented, notably having said his business had recognised that there existed 'a vast reading public for intelligent books at low prices' (Lane, 1938a, p. 969).

What this and other similar statements gave rise to was a riff on the general reader label, whereby an adjectival prefix would often be added, one that would have the effect of modifying rather meaningfully the parameters of Penguin's target audience: 'the intelligent general reader',[12] which Rylance (2005, p. 59) refers to as a 'long-established Penguin formula and target readership'. By extension, of course, we must read this to mean that Lane, and indeed Penguin, concurrently recognised the existence of somewhat less intelligent general readers, and that their books therefore cannot possibly have been meant for just any general reader after all. And if we needed further confirmation, Bill Williams provides it whilst writing *The Penguin Story* to celebrate the company's twenty-first birthday. Williams was then the editor of Penguin's Pelican list, and he became so closely associated with the Pelicans' unexpected success that he became affectionately known as 'Pelican Bill'. In a chapter looking to the Penguin business's future potential, entitled 'Penguin Prospect', Williams (1956, p. 58) states: 'The Penguin market, despite its ten million sales, is not a mass market, and the firm never intends to seek a truly mass market. Its books, especially outside crime and detection, are deliberately designed to appeal to a readership which probably does not exceed one-tenth of the population.'

In short, Williams admits that a mass-market approach was neither the intention nor the reality. Unfortunately, Williams does not give more detail as to the particular profile of the one-tenth of the population he cites, but by now we can barely escape the implication. Scholars, indeed, have described with regularity Penguin's dichotomy of intention/statement vs reality as 'having a slightly middlebrow edge to it' (Collini, 2012, p. 659; see also

---

[12] There are many examples of this phrase in use, such as in the 'Notes for Editors' of the Penguin English Library (Hare, 1995, p. 297). Perhaps most telling of its widespread use is not so much its adoption by Penguin staff but in the attempts of would-be Penguin authors to style their works as appropriate for 'the intelligent general reader', such as Lyons (2013, pp. 69–70) shows was true of John M. Allegro who translated the Dead Sea Scrolls for Penguin in 1957.

Humble, 2011, p. 57). Certainly, this would fit rather neatly with the aspirational, upwardly mobile readers of Penguins whom we have just encountered. Even Clement Attlee is reported to have admitted to J. E. Morpurgo that 'his path to Downing Street was paved with Penguins' (Wood, 1985, p. 36). We might well ask, therefore, whether it was precisely the likes of Cannadine, Hoggart and Bradbury of whom Williams was thinking when he offered this assessment. It seems likely.

So far in this discussion of the identity of the general reader, we have not homed in, except in passing, on the series with which this Element is concerned, Penguin Classics, rather maintaining a more general overview of Penguin and the type of reader for whom it was established. It would be a generalisation, but not entirely inaccurate, to say that a similar story is also true for Classics, though Classics clearly also achieved an identity of its own. I stated earlier that nowhere do we hear more about our general reader than in relation to Classics; given the previous discussion, in some ways this is the oddest part of Penguin's self-imposed positioning in the marketplace. Other early Penguins, of course, could broadly be classified as contemporary, or at least relatively recent, examples of quality literary fiction; at least in principle, such books might hope to appeal to a fairly broad audience. The early Classics, by contrast, led the reader into new and unfamiliar worlds: they were English translations of ancient Greek and Latin texts, the appeal of which seems unlikely to have been a hook for drawing in an especially wide readership. The fact that *The Odyssey* sold as many copies as it did, of course, suggests the book did find a large audience – but large in number does not necessarily equate to wide in demographics. Penguin's insistence on its products' place as books for the general reader, both in retrospect and in general, thus seems pretty suspect. This is particularly strange if we think about the market that had, in the end, embraced Penguins more generally: the Hoggarts, Bradburys and Cannadines of the world. If, thanks to changing class relations and access to education, an intellectually energetic market had been proven for Penguin's products, why then would Penguin shy away from targeting it explicitly once it had created a book series that had that very market written all over it?

Penguin's was not the first attempt to create commercial returns in the 'translation of classic texts' business: other houses had done just that, but their success had been limited. It was one thing to issue versions of great English writers' works from centuries past, but to do so for those of the ancient world must have seemed to many of Lane's colleagues an audacious idea too far. Indeed, Rieu, a retired publisher of school textbooks whom Lane had met at a party, did not even have the profile for a job such as this (Morpurgo, 1979, p. 215). I suggest, however, that it is precisely in Rieu's leadership – which lasted until 1964 – that we can identify the principles upon which the series was initially founded, and afterwards at least partially governed, regardless of the eventual readers that Classics actually reached. After all, whilst Rieu was educated as an undergraduate at Balliol College, Oxford, he was not an academic by profession and, as we saw Bill Williams (1956, p. 19) earlier describe: 'Rieu's object was to break away from the academic idiom in which so many of the world's classics have been put before the general reader, and to present them in contemporary English without any transgressions of scholarship or textual inaccuracy.' Rieu was resolute, then, that this was not an academic enterprise – these books should categorically not be obfuscated by the typical paradigms of scholarly style that in his view alienated potential reading audiences outside of the academy. As he put it, his Penguins would be 'shorn of the unnecessary difficulties and erudition, the archaic flavour and the foreign idiom that renders so many existing translations repellent to modern taste' (Rieu, 1946, p. 48).

This, however, seems not necessarily to have been the view amongst some of Rieu's later colleagues, such as the notoriously abrasive Tony Godwin (the 'half-educated young upstart', who apparently called Rieu, in return, the 'Edwardian old fogey' (Hare, 1995, p. 189)) and the rather more diplomatic Betty Radice, who both worked on Classics during the 1960s. Godwin and Radice, as well as others, are documented to have been aware of a burgeoning educational market for Classics, and their attempts to get Rieu to recognise this were often frustrated (Hare, 1995, p. 189). Even upon his retirement, Rieu would still maintain that he 'designed [the Classics] to give pleasure even more than instruction' (Rieu quoted in Hare, 2008a, p. 31). I will return to Radice, Godwin and their contemporaries in more detail later, especially when I come to discuss the particular medieval French Penguin Classics that will form the central case studies of this

Element. For now, it suffices to say that Radice's and Godwin's eventual success in deliberately tapping into education-related markets has sometimes given the impression that 'an educational project' had been at the heart of Classics from the outset (see e.g. Boll, 2016, p. 33; McAteer, 2017, pp. 50–4). Book reviews, even those appearing within the first twenty years of the Classics' appearance in the marketplace, provide incontrovertible evidence of this, such as that by Margaret Getty (1955) for *Phoenix*, in which she lauds the series in general but makes abundantly clear her assumption that the books are meant for educational practice when she inserts a closing plea:

> As soon as possible, opportunity should be taken to remedy one serious defect. With some honourable exceptions, no references or page-headings have been provided to the original text. This is particularly disconcerting for teachers who wish to use the series to illustrate lectures, and who constantly need to verify passages in the original author.
> (p. 129)

The very fact that Classics came to occupy such a vaunted position, and indeed that Godwin and Radice conceived of them in that way from their earliest contact with them, probably was – despite his lofty intentions of avoiding anything approaching academic – a platform of Rieu's own making, as was also true of Lane before him. In spite of Rieu's and Lane's vehement opposition to an academic pedigree for the Classics ('they harboured no thoughts on the valuable teaching materials they were providing' (Pratt, 2008a, p. 13)), with Rieu in particular having reportedly told his son that he had found very few 'dons [who] could write decent English' (Radice, 1987, p. 21; Hare, 2008a, p. 26; Boll, 2016, p. 39), both men somewhat ironically ended up having to surround themselves with academic authors and translators from the very earliest stages of Classics, precisely because of the advanced linguistic skill set needed to produce the works (McAteer, 2017, p. 53; Wood, 1985, p. 26; Boll, 2016, p. 39). Radice would continue this afterwards, too, consulting academics as a matter of course about translations from languages she did not know

(Radice, 1987, p. 20). In other words, non-academics were rarely in possession of either the time or the skills needed to produce such a text, so academics frequently ended up being involved in the process of bringing a Classic to market. Just how involved academics were is a subject to which I will return in Section 3, but it suffices to say here that even if inherent academic rigour was not a claim upon which Classics deliberately traded, the evidence suggests that academics arguably had a fair stake in the endeavour.

Other Penguin series would be less apologetic about the types of readers for whom their books were primarily crafted. For example, founded in 1937, just a few years prior to Classics in 1944, were the Pelicans, apparently so-named after Lane overheard a lady mistakenly asking after Pelicans rather than Penguins in a bookshop. Lane, as we have seen, had a knack of 'turning accidents into policy' (Morpurgo, 1979, p. 118); even before he had had a chance to think what a Pelican book might look like, so the story goes, he contacted his lawyer to safeguard the name, apparently concerned that if someone else used it, they would be 'stealing my thunder' (unpublished interview of Lane by Heather Mansell, quoted in Penguin Books, 1985, pp. 25–6). Lane's editorial advisors suggested that the time was ripe to publish '"serious" books, breaking the convention of reprinting works already published by other houses, and publishing specially commissioned titles straight into paperback on subjects of interest to "the intelligent layman"' (Penguin Books, 1985, p. 26).

As it would turn out, the early Pelicans did end up being reprints of a range of non-fiction titles, but original commissions soon followed. In advertising them, Lane (1938b, p. 42) continued to tout the Penguin mantra that even Pelicans were fodder for a broad readership, 'a thirsty public', as he called them, whose supposed 'popular taste' was a fiction. In a similar piece from the same year, Lane (1938a, p. 969) found an alternative way to invoke the general reader by describing Pelican Classics as 'the true everyman's library of the twentieth century, covering the whole range of arts and sciences and bringing the finest products of modern thought and art to the people'. One might even question whether Lane was taking a bold swipe at rival publisher, Everyman's Library, with this statement.

By contrast, however, and despite their usual generalising statements about the identity of their readership, Penguin's own company histories seem proud to proclaim for whom Pelicans were intended from the very outset: 'When the first Pelicans were published the intention behind them was to provide the serious general reader with authoritative books on a wide range of intellectual interests' (Williams, 1956, pp. 14–15). Indeed, Williams continues by remarking that by the time of his writing on the occasion of Penguin's twenty-first birthday, the audience had extended far beyond just the 'intelligent layman'. Yet again, however, this was not an especially diverse demographic. Pelicans became, he says, 'such a library: and one serving, moreover, not only the general reader of serious purpose, but also the great body of students pursuing courses in the Universities and institutions of higher education generally' (p. 15).

This is one of the earliest references I have found to an outward-facing acknowledgement, one coming from within the walls of Penguin at a relatively early stage, that a student audience, an academic audience, was known to exist for the books that Penguin produced. This, however, seems to have been typical of Williams, who was 'an inspiring evangelist for the democratisation of British culture' (Laity, 2014). In a letter to Victor Weybright dated 6 March 1946, for example, Williams described publishing as 'a vocation as well as a trade' and thus that Penguin could fairly claim to be 'public educators' (Hare, 1995, p. 306). Later, he would even go so far as to link the establishment of Pelicans to what he called 'the current crusade in education' (Hare, 1995, p. 52).

Other references to intellectually minded readers would appear when Penguin launched its Penguin English Library in 1963. Even then, though, despite the very fact that the series would contain explanatory notes and glosses – paratexts more usually aimed at an academic reader – the official 'Notes for Editors' insisted '[t]he audience to aim at is the intelligent general reader who always meant to read the English Classics, but has either never got round to all of these or at least not looked at them since his school days' (Hare, 1995, p. 297). An educated audience, then, but not the academic one specifically singled out by Williams for Pelicans – and still, the term 'general' remains attached. George Donaldson (2013, p. 121) has shown, however, just how revealing archival research can be in discovering the truth behind these kinds of statements, for his enquiry into the 'principles and policies that impelled' the Penguin English Library to market shows that behind closed doors, Penguin actually had in mind to target *both* the general reader and 'academics and students' at the same time: neither one on its own, Penguin thought, could ensure financial viability. Of course, though, how distinct each of these actually is from the other remains a matter for debate.

Regardless of how open these two series were in respect of divulging the academic credentials of their audiences, though, there can be no denying that in establishing these lists, Penguin to some extent accepted and, indeed, embraced its role as an educator. In respect of Classics, however, Penguin continued to shrink away from admitting the same, even where archival evidence strongly suggests that Classics served as a model for Penguin's subsequent and more explicitly educational series: the Penguin English Library was, for instance, initially called 'Penguin English Classics' (Donaldson, 2013, p. 117). As a means of securing its commercial success, Penguin deliberately appointed David Daiches of the University of Sussex to serve as both series editor and editor of the series' first volume, to emulate Rieu's role for Classics (Hare, 1995, p. 297).[13] As alluded to earlier, though, Classics continued to be marketed resolutely for many decades at the general reader, sometimes the 'intelligent general reader', but never the academic reader. To some degree, this still holds true today, with the Penguin Classics UK official web pages (www.penguin.co.uk/penguin-classics) offering no hint whatsoever that these books are suitable for any particular reader. It also does not mention the general reader; but by saying nothing at all, Penguin UK appears tacitly to imply that these are books meant for anyone. Of course, this cannot possibly be an accurate representation of Penguin's market understanding, as modern marketing practice prohibits such imprecision, and data gathering and mining are now so advanced that Penguin UK has a great deal of consumer insight to help it understand who is reading and purchasing its books: leaving it unsaid is a deliberate choice. The US Penguin Classics web pages (www.penguin.com/classics, see 'About' section), by contrast, offer a far deeper analysis of the Classics market, suggesting that 'the importance of the academic market, particularly in the United States', driven by the

---

[13] Daiches, however, would subsequently resign from the post on a matter of policy (Hare, 1995, p. 297).

expansion of the universities, 'was fully recognized during the 1960s'. I will return to the importance and influence of Penguin's US operation in Section 3, but this evidence alone suggests that Penguin US may have been more aware of an academic readership than its head office in the United Kingdom.[14] Why might this be?

This question is especially pertinent when one considers that whilst Rieu was not an academic, his successors, Robert Baldick and Betty Radice, most certainly were. Radice, a Classics scholar and tutor, worked directly with Rieu as his assistant from 1959, before becoming (upon Rieu's retirement) the joint editor of Classics with Baldick, a fellow of Pembroke College, Oxford. Rieu's retirement had very likely been (at least partially) driven by an increased tension between him and Godwin, who had joined the senior editorial group of Penguin in 1960, rising shortly afterwards to the position of chief editor (Hare, 1995, pp. 188–9; Crowe, 2012, p. 207). Whilst Radice's approach, knowing the burgeoning academic market as she did, was to make considered change steadily, Godwin seemed to be moving at a more accelerated speed. In a particularly furious note from April 1963, Rieu asked Lane how he could allow someone, 'without discussion with me, its editor, to mutilate [the] series' and reminded him of their agreement that Rieu would continue as editor for five more years (Hare, 1995, p. 189). Just nine months later, Rieu retired. However, he does not seem to have stormed out of the building in a fit of anger but rather to have been persuaded that while his successors, Radice and Baldick, would introduce change, they would look after the series with care and do so, to some degree, in his image. In his 1964 retirement speech, he predicted 'a long and prosperous life for [Classics] . . . And it is because I have worked with my two successors, Mrs Betty Radice and Dr Baldick, that I speak with such confidence' (quoted in Radice, 1987, p. 10; see also Hare, 1995, p. 190).

---

[14] As a related aside, the debates around the imperatives for linking citizenship and reading that we encountered earlier in post-war Britain are slightly different in the American Cold War context, but nonetheless present. For example, Joanne P. Sharp (2000) sets out how the *Reader's Digest* operated as a 'voice' for 'mass' culture, as evidenced by its marketing, during the Cold War.

Indeed, in this same speech, Rieu seems also to have reconciled himself to his series' educational value, and that the time was ripe for fresh eyes:

> The Penguin Classics, though I designed them to give pleasure even more than instruction, have been hailed as the greatest educative force of the twentieth century. And far be it for me to quarrel with that encomium, for there is no one whom they have educated more than myself.
> (Quoted in Pratt, 2008b, p. 31)

Radice's achievement in getting Rieu to warm to her editorial plans might legitimately be attributed to her wider ability to serve as a mediator, a voice of balance, something she had become rather skilled at thanks to her refereeing of the frictions between Rieu and Godwin (Hare, 1995, p. 189). On the one hand, she clearly appreciated and acknowledged Rieu's objectives and his skill. Indeed, Radice's son, William, would later disclose that whilst Radice and Rieu had their differences, 'she had the highest possible regard for him, and in their common modesty, domesticity and liking for plants, children and animals . . . as well as their professional interests, they were soul-mates' (Radice, 1987, pp. 17–18).

What Rieu had tried to achieve with Classics was thus by no means lost on Radice. On the other hand, she also took a pragmatic view of what needed to change. In talking of the academic audience for Classics in an undated internal memorandum, she said:

> This was not in the mind of the founder of the series, who thought of something enjoyable for the 'general reader' and met with a certain amount of criticism from the academic world; the idea of a 'crib' was somewhat disreputable. Now we know that the Classics are widely used in teaching, and they must be 'useful' as well as enjoyable.
> (Quoted in Hare, 1995, p. 189)

Here, Radice seems to suggest that she recognised the need to strike a balance. She was cheerfully working in the shadow of, or at least with respect for, Rieu and so would continue to equip the Classics with the tools to be enjoyable for, and marketable to, wider audiences (even if they rarely reached them) whilst ensuring that they also contained the apparatus that would make them work for the academic audiences they had found. Indeed, Radice (1969) made a particularly impassioned defence of the premise of Classics and the series' development in a response to D. S. Carne-Ross's (1968) rather critical report on Penguin Classics' first two decades, published in *Arion*. Radice (1969, p. 136) admits wondering if it is always possible to balance 'being scholarly without being pedantic' or, in other words, to square the reality of the market with Rieu's vision, but she does not confess to being at all perturbed by this, rather warm to 'the challenge' (p. 132). Given this context, it is perhaps unsurprising that Classics in the UK context would be more reluctant to admit its status openly as books for academics than they would in the United States. Nonetheless, there can be no doubt that Penguins were received, on both sides of the Atlantic, in that capacity, as we will see later.

Perhaps the starkest evidence that the general reader campaign became, in the end, a veil with which to cover (thinly) the Classics' real readership is provided by a poll carried out in 2015 by the Academic Book of the Future Project,[15] a research project jointly funded by the Arts and Humanities Research Council and the British Library, which ran between 2014 and 2016. The poll, a core activity undertaken during the inaugural (now annual) Academic Book Week, asked participants, all of whom came from the book trade, to submit titles that they believed should find a place on the 'Top 20 academic books that changed the world' list. More than 200 titles were submitted, and a panel of book trade experts invited by the Booksellers' Association was asked to choose twenty from amongst them to make up the final list. Of the twenty chosen,[16] just one (Germaine Greer's

---

[15] For the poll, see https://acbookweek.com/20booksbywomenthatchangedtheworld/20abcworld/, and for the project, see https://academicbookfuture.org.

[16] The 'Top 20' books were *A Brief History of Time* by Stephen Hawking, *A Vindication of the Rights of Woman* by Mary Wollstonecraft, *Critique of Pure Reason* by Immanuel Kant, *Nineteen Eighty-Four* by George Orwell, *On the Origin of Species* by Charles Darwin, *Orientalism* by Edward Said, *Silent Spring*

The Female Eunuch) had not been published at some point in its history by Penguin (in all but two cases the rest were published as Classics or Modern Classics, the latter being a series founded by Godwin in 1961 to have a similar remit to Classics, but focusing on contemporary literature). This in itself says something important, first, about the power of a Penguin book to influence, and to take a role in canon formation, a subject to which I return in Section 2.2. Second, and more importantly, however, is that the poll reveals these books being formally classified, and by individuals knowledgeable about the book trade, as academic books. Of course, it makes sense that some of these titles should be categorised so, such as Charles Darwin's *On the Origin of Species* (the eventual winner) or Stephen Hawking's *A Brief History of Time*. The latter is a crossover book, admittedly, but it is nonetheless obviously a form of scholarly output. Whether the same can be said of George Orwell's *Nineteen Eighty-Four* and the *Complete Works* of Shakespeare is a matter for debate.

It is not within the remit of this Element to have that debate here, but the choices of books in the poll do raise several important questions. If the vast majority of these books were published at some point by Penguin, does that go some way to explaining their appearance in this list? The widely varied generic categories of the titles suggest, at the very least, that it is not simply the case that Penguin happens to select, consciously or otherwise, acutely academic texts. Put another way, can we take this poll as evidence that Penguin's association with the academy has become so tightly intermeshed that the mere inclusion of a title on Classics in some way instils in public consciousness not merely that it is an important book but also that it is an academic one? Are Classics, therefore, not just books suitable for

by Rachel Carson, *The Communist Manifesto* by Karl Marx and Friedrich Engels, *The Complete Works* by William Shakespeare, *The Female Eunuch* by Germaine Greer, *The Making of the English Working Class* by E. P. Thompson, *The Meaning of Relativity* by Albert Einstein, *The Naked Ape* by Desmond Morris, *The Prince* by Niccolò Machiavelli, *The Republic* by Plato, *The Rights of Man* by Thomas Paine, *The Second Sex* by Simone de Beauvoir, *The Uses of Literacy* by Richard Hoggart, *The Wealth of Nations* by Adam Smith and *Ways of Seeing* by John Berger.

academics but also books that are perceived as academic in their very essence? This poll certainly seems to suggest so, especially since it is one whose participants should be well placed enough professionally to distinguish between academic and non-academic titles (again, they are demonstrably not general readers), unlike a non-specialist public, who could perhaps be forgiven for greater confusion in the matter. And if the Classics brand has become so unavoidably linked to the academy, then what concrete evidence exists to help us to understand better why that is so? I have already alluded to some of the more circumstantial reasons as to why this might have happened, and my enquiry into Classics' medieval French translations will provide tangible evidence from the Penguin Archive in respect of specific titles and their routes to market that will help to elucidate this further. Before I do that, however, I would like to pause briefly to consider whether the concept of a 'classic' may in itself have something to do with Penguin Classics' relationship with 'the literary canon' (to use a notoriously divisive term) and therefore, by extension, with the academy.

2.2 What Makes a Classic a Classic, and What Connects Classics to the Academy?

Since we have established that Penguin Classics are so widely perceived as academic (or at least academic-related) titles, I want to explore briefly how a title acquires the status of a 'classic' and thus, often, a place in the so-called literary canon. Higher education institutions have of course, and until relatively recently, advocated largely for teaching 'classic texts' or 'the traditional canon' in their literary programmes, thus typically avoiding (consciously and unconsciously) both more marginal and more diverse titles. Debates and campaigns are gradually helping to change this.[17] Nonetheless, an intrinsic connection between classic texts, the canon and the academy remains. I want to ask whether academic conceptions of the canon may have, unconsciously or otherwise, influenced Penguin's choices

[17] See, for example, Macaluso and Macaluso (2018), Fernández-Armesto (2018) and curricula diversifying projects such as the University of Edinburgh's Project Myopia, www.projectmyopia.com, and the 'Why is my curriculum white?' campaign founded at University College London.

for publication of Classics, or if Penguin's mere selection of a text for Classics has, in some cases, earned it entry into the 'canon', thus fuelling a kind of unconscious perception of a relationship with the academy. Have Classics in themselves, indeed, come to constitute a kind of literary canon, and is that perhaps amongst the reasons why Penguin, despite its best efforts, never really found a true home with the general reader, being rather more comfortable in an academic setting? What cannot be included here, because of scope, is a discussion of what does and/or should constitute the literary canon: that work has been done elsewhere by other scholars.[18]

So what counts as a classic? Of course, there have been various attempts to define it, starting with T. S. Eliot's 1945 essay 'What is a classic?' published by Faber. Eliot argued for the existence of two kinds of classic, the first being 'the universal classic' which has importance beyond its time, place and language, and the classic which is only 'such in relation to the other literature in its own language, or according to the view of life of a particular period' (Eliot, 1957, p. 54). Both kinds of classic, however, he links to a sense of maturity: 'A classic', he says:

> can only occur when a civilization is mature; when a language and a literature are mature; and it must be the work of a mature mind. It is the importance of that civilization and of that language, as well as the comprehensiveness of the mind of the individual poet, which gives the universality.
> (pp. 54–5)

Eliot thus gives a sense that a classic is a text that represents a kind of durability or, as J. M. Coetzee (1993, p. 20) interprets Eliot's core definition, '[t]he classic defines itself by surviving.' Coetzee qualifies this by adding that attacks on a classic are therefore welcome because once the text proves

---

[18] A particularly helpful summary is provided by Roche (2004), and a further update is provided by Papadima, Damrosch and d'Haen (2011); other studies, amongst the many, include Guillory (1995); Kolbas (2001); Gorak (1991). Perhaps most seminal in sparking modern debate on the matter is Bloom (1994).

itself no longer to need protection from such attacks, it has truly reached the status of a classic.

Frank Kermode makes a particularly seminal contribution to the topic of the classic, and it is one which also uses Eliot as the point of departure, similarly suggesting that longevity is at the heart of defining a classic text. Kermode, however, takes the argument a step further by suggesting that classics are books that are able to maintain a kind of sense of modernity through their constant reinterpretation (Kermode, 1975; see also Kermode, 1976). That is, they endure through adaptation. Kermode, then, draws a distinction between texts that do not work out of their time, similar in a way to Eliot's classic that is not universal, and those that endure because they can be reimagined by new generations. This definition is what leads William Radice (2008, p. 5) to position the Penguin Classics imprint as an important contributor to the classic status of the texts it publishes, because of Classics' agency in (re-)translating such titles and thus opening them up to reinterpretation by new generations.

Martin Yates (2008) points out that the Penguin Classic actually requires more specific definition than this, because he counts around twenty varieties of Classic. However, despite this promising opening, the nearest that Yates gets in offering a definition for what constitutes a Penguin Classic is to say that 'this book has been around for a long while and deserves to be taken seriously' (p. 33). In respect of the twenty varieties of Penguin Classic to which Yates refers, it transpires that Yates is less interested in offering insights into their differing conceptual design(s) than in documenting their changing visual identity, particularly cover designs.[19] Nonetheless, despite

---

[19] Whilst the Classics' changing visual identity is not at the core of the current discussion, it is worth noting the broad changes in cover design that happened during the period under discussion in Section 3 of this Element. They are the 'Medallion Classics', which were launched with *The Odyssey* in 1946 (so-named as each had its own 'specially drawn medallion device on the cover' (Yates, 2008, p. 33)); these were also referred to as Roundels (Schmoller, 2008) and ran until 1963 when the covers were given a distinctive black background. 'Black Classics', as they came to be known, then relaunched in 1985 with a new design, featuring a beige background and colour banding for different languages (Yates, 2008, pp. 33–4).

the sense of unity applied to the physical design of Classics (i.e. that all Classics have the same template until the next rebrand), Yates's more general point that Classics come in different varieties remains salient. This is especially pertinent because in 1986, Penguin Classics, a list for classic works of fiction in translation, merged with the Penguin English Library, Pelican Classics and the Penguin American Library. This merger meant that literary, historical and non-fiction texts all sat alongside one another under the umbrella of Classics, creating 'the most comprehensive library of world literature available from any paperback publisher' (Pratt 2008a, p. 30). In some ways, it is surprising that the merger did not happen sooner, since Betty Radice is documented in correspondence with Moses Finley (editor of Pelican Classics) from 1968 to have rallied strongly against the notion that texts should be pigeonholed into genres, particularly in such a way as to designate them 'non-literary'. Taking the examples of St Augustine's *Confessions* and Sir Thomas More's *Utopia*, which were being threatened with a move to Pelican, Radice states: 'such books can be read for many reasons and in many contexts, but they are undeniably [also] great works of literature' (Radice to Finlay, 17 August 1968, quoted in Hare, 1995, p. 304).

Even if Yates does not muse on the distinctions between Classics, something in his broad generalisation warrants a moment's pause. To paraphrase, a Penguin Classic is a book that *deserves to be taken seriously*. Yates thus seems to suggest that in being chosen for Classics, a book has been given a kind of seal of approval. It is a warrant that the text is one that, to return to the thinking of Kermode and Eliot, has endured both time and adversity and has safely emerged on the other side. This, to some degree, echoes the words of Bradbury (1985, p. 8) quoted earlier, where he states that he would scrupulously note which texts Penguin chose to publish and which it did not, for that would guide him in his reading choices by indicating what *should* be on his list of 'must-reads'. For Bradbury, this is what constitutes Penguin's true achievement: 'the endless extension of the canon of reading' (Bradbury, 1985, p. 8). In Bradbury's view, therefore, Penguin not only recognises and publishes 'the canon', a point also echoed by Sanders (2013, p. 114), but the Penguin list in itself came to constitute a kind of canon. In other words, it served (and serves) as a guide for readers as to what they should be reading, thus operating in a mode rather less akin to a set of recommendations for enjoyable reads, and more like a prescriptive university reading list. Bradbury's additional comment that Penguin's 'huge list of titles in print makes up a vast modern university' completes the circle.[20] If Penguin Classics have an effect on, and indeed create, a canon, then the list cannot avoid being perceived in the same way as are other circumscribed canons of reading, such as university reading lists: such canons are *constructions*; they are human-made (often with the emphasis on 'man', as Don Paterson alluded to in the 2018 Stevenson Lecture (annual lecture in memory of Professor Iain Stevenson), during which he described canons as 'blokey constructions').[21] To put it another way: since an impression is created that Penguin built – consciously or otherwise[22] – a kind of canon of reading, what inevitably results is the spectre of an educated, largely male elite telling people (often other men, as shown in Section 2.1) what constitutes quality and what does not, and therefore what they should and should not read – a situation deeply reminiscent of that in higher education, particularly in the mid-twentieth century.[23] In this sense, it is not hard to understand this as another likely reason why Penguin

---

[20] Bradbury is far from the only critic to refer to Penguin's list as a university; see, for example, Laity (2014) who describes Penguins as 'a kind of home university for an army of autodidacts, aspirant culture-vultures and social radicals'.

[21] With thanks to Samantha Rayner for this quotation.

[22] In support of the notion that Penguin's list may, in some way, have been a conscious attempt at a kind of canon formation is Bill Williams's (1956, p. 60) comment in Penguin's twenty-first anniversary volume, which states: 'the freelance phase of Penguins is over; the adventurous sallies have given way to the solid responsibility of building up a comprehensive Popular Educator. The fulfilment of this function is now one of the primary objectives of Penguin Books.' Whether this really was a 'primary objective' of Penguin Books is, as we have seen, highly debatable. Williams may well be confusing his own *modus operandi* as Pelican editor with that of the company as a whole.

[23] It is important to remember, though, that whatever the outward impression created, a great number of women were integral cogs in the Penguin machine, not least Betty Radice. Rebecca E. Lyons's previously mentioned Element will reveal more on this topic.

Classics, despite Rieu's initial intentions, found itself so closely associated with the academy.

Indeed, despite Penguin's various outward-facing attempts to avoid the association, this connection of the academy to Penguin through prescribed canons of reading was actually galvanised at an early stage. By the mid-1950s, the combination of affordability and the perception of Penguin as a publisher that published 'canonical' texts meant that Classics were appearing as 'ancillaries in courses at universities and institutions of higher education', and at least 50 per cent of those sold in the United States 'were supplied to campus bookstores' (De Bellaigue, 2001a, p. 75). In the United Kingdom, too, despite the (intelligent) general reader agenda touted by Penguin, titles from the Penguin English Library would find 'their way into educational syllabuses' almost immediately from the moment of its launch in 1963 (Rylance, 2005, p. 59).

Radice, we have come to understand, increasingly noticed the growing demand and – as alluded to earlier – sought to ensure that while each Classic had to remain accessible, it also had to have the right apparatus to enable its use in scholarship; she therefore quietly began updating existing titles with fuller notes, updated bibliographies and expert introductions (Pratt, 2008b, pp. 28, 31), even sometimes having the translations themselves redone (Hare, 1995, p. 304), as will be touched upon later in relation to Dorothy Sayers's and Glyn Burgess's translations of *The Song of Roland*. Rylance (2005, p. 59) even reports that 'new and old university campuses were trawled for aspirant academics eager to reform the intellectual agenda and turn a shapely sentence between strongly coloured covers.'

Whether Penguin was actually as proactive as Rylance suggests in courting academics in this way is something that I will consider in Section 3, but for now it is enough to say that even though both internal and external circumvention of the university link continued, the association had become practically impossible to elude by the late 1960s. For example, the apparently burgeoning Penguin canon gave rise to rather frequent comparisons of Penguin with the university presses of Oxford and Cambridge. Williams (1956, p. 29), for instance, proudly notes that Penguin ran 'neck-and-neck' with them in design competitions while, in an interview with *The Listener* on 28 January 1971, Godwin (quoted in Hare, 1995, p. 254) advocated that there were two imprints 'that mean something to the public' – Oxford University Press and Penguin Classics. Undoubtedly important, though possibly accidental, in Penguin's reluctant assumption of the role of 'supplier of set texts to the higher education market' was the Robbins Report of 1963, in which the university sector was earmarked for expansion, particularly in Penguin's key areas of the arts and social sciences. The recommendations of the Robbins Report took effect almost immediately and the eventual expansion of higher education far exceeded both intention and aspiration since, by 1980, student numbers in the United Kingdom had increased by 770 per cent as opposed to the projected 400 percent (Rylance, 2005, p. 61). We will see up close some of the tangible effects of the expansion of universities in Section 3.

Towards the end of Allen Lane's life (he died of colon cancer on 7 July 1970), it seems he may have made peace with the notion that Penguin Books, and Classics in particular, had become standard texts – even that they set a standard – for those engaged in scholarly pursuits. Lane was an admirer of the BBC, comparing its precepts to 'educate as well as entertain' to Penguin's own founding principles in his Chairman's Statement of 18 April 1962 (quoted in Hare, 1995, p. 306). When the BBC then stated that 'Penguin Books have been the greatest popular educators in our generation', Lane proclaimed it to be the greatest compliment he had ever been paid (Wood, 1985, p. 36), indicating his acceptance of the position in serious education that his books had earned. Indeed, he is widely reported to have claimed that Classics in particular were his proudest achievement (Pratt, 2008a, p. 30). And perhaps we should not be surprised that the Classics link with the academy had become more palatable to Lane. The expansion of higher education, after all, actually spoke to the very principles upon which he had founded Penguin in the first place. No longer was university to be the realm of the elite; it would be open to a wider demographic, at the core of which was an ideal of offering education and cultural benefit to the people, objectives close to Lane's heart. Debates swirling around the Robbins Report would surely have angered Lane in their opposition to the things he stood for: many counterarguments were entrenched, for example, in questions of threats to standards; of dumbing down; and of 'the wanton production of an unnecessary, greedy, feckless, dissatisfied, over-educated, unemployable segment of the population' (Rylance, 2005, p. 61). This may well explain why Lane, in the year before his death, attempted to gather a consortium of universities to sustain the Penguin cultural agenda. He would sell his shares to them at a fair rate as a means of linking state education with a commercial concern. Unfortunately, universities could promise neither to guarantee against losses nor never to sell off the shares in times of financial difficulty, so the endeavour failed (Rylance, 2005, pp. 61–2). It may also have been this proposal to link Penguin to universities formally that gave rise to a poster with the curious heading 'The Penguin University', which can be seen in the background of a photo of Penguin collector Steve Hare, printed in the *Metro* newspaper, and which can still be viewed in the online version (Smith, 2010).[24]

Even if it would not be a university consortium that would ensure the future of Penguin, the day after Lane's death the company was acquired by the established educational publisher Pearson-Longman, thereby affirming that the seeming 'educational character' of Penguin was in fact less seeming and rather more definite (De Bellaigue, 2001c, p. 220). The evidence suggests, then, that even if Penguin would continue to describe its core market as one outside of formal education, it had finally admitted to itself that education and entertainment did not have to be mutually exclusive, even in the case of Penguin Classics. Having dual objectives was workable: on the one hand, Penguin could strive to create quality book products that readers could enjoy, and this would remain the core *raison d'être* in the company's public-facing operation; on the other, Penguin could quietly accept and cultivate its connection with the academy. Penguin Classics, thanks in chief to Betty Radice's foresight, was the perfect vehicle for achieving this balance, since their careful refocusing under Radice's guidance chimed particularly well with the fact that 'the distinction between

---

[24] Attempts to discover the provenance of this poster have been unsuccessful to date – but given the 1960s typography and style, it is not impossible that it may have served as some kind of promotional material when Lane was courting vice chancellors. Alternatively, it may refer to the kind of 'home university' stocked with Penguins that Hare would later speak about when interviewed by *The Guardian* (Laity, 2014).

informing and teaching had been gradually breaking down for years' (Hare, 1995, p. 306). As this Element has shown repeatedly, Radice was far from alone in recognising where Classics needed to go,[25] namely to acquire, as Hare (2006, p. 55) suggests, 'a constant foot in the door of the educational establishment'. However, a conundrum remains in relation to the company, and the series, at large. If Penguin Classics only truly recognised its market, and even then reluctantly, once the expansion of universities was well under way, why did the imprint turn its attention in the late 1950s away from the likes of Shakespeare and Virgil, authors at least recognisable if not accessible to the average anglophone audience, to continental medieval authors who really could not, even with the best will in the world, be widely known? For whom would the likes of Chrétien de Troyes and the anonymous author of the *Song of Roland* be of interest? Taking Classics' medieval French literary titles as a series of case studies, Section 3 will attempt to answer this question, as well as to offer more concrete evidence from the Penguin Archive that sheds light on Penguin Classics' actual working relationships with both the general reader and the academy. Owing to its nature as a series of archival-based case studies, it will also provide helpful, tangible evidence of some of the ways in which Penguin, and British publishers more generally, surfed the waves of the changing sociocultural environment in the post-war period, which speaks to existing historiographical debates such as Christopher Hilliard's (2006) reconstruction of the social dynamics that led to an explosion of creative writing amongst the lower social classes in the interwar period, Jonathan Rose's (2001) rather optimistic arguments in favour of the working classes' constant aspiration and voracious reading of all kinds of literature in the early twentieth century, or Selina Todd's (2014) more nuanced reading and meticulous mining of the reading habits of the general reader.

---

[25] As one example, Michael Grant (1960, pp. 19–20) would similarly question why 'popularizing' had to be distinct from 'research', as 'without research there will be nothing to popularize [and] good popularization in this generation may, by the spark which it lights in a few of its many readers, mean new scholarly advances in the next.'

3 Publishing Medieval French Literature as Penguin Classics

3.1 Gathering Steam: 1956–1979

Whilst the first medieval French Penguin Classic would not appear until 1957, in fact it was as early as 1944 that plans were afoot for French translations, presumably including medieval, modern and anything in between, to join the Classics. A letter from Rieu to Lane on 19 October of that year sets out his broader plans for the Classics series, amongst which, he said: 'I am also considering a French list' (quoted in Hare, 1995, p. 186). We can probably assume that Rieu's long-term plan would be to draw classic texts out of all languages and bring them to an anglophone readership; however, in this letter we see that his priorities lie, first of all, with some 'forty Greek and Roman authors', followed by the proposed French list and perhaps 'one or two Scandinavian translations ... in particular Ibsen's plays'. What Rieu does not mention is *why* these should be the focus of his endeavours, other than that his ideas have arisen following consultation with friends.

In this section, I explore the routes to market of Penguin's medieval French literary titles to see if the rationale underlying their publication, as documented in the Penguin Archive at the University of Bristol, provides corroboration for Section 2's findings in respect of Penguin's relationship with the general reader and the academy. I am aware that in referring to the titles with which I am concerned as 'literary', I may sound as if I am drawing a debatable generic line, especially when discussing texts such as Froissart's *Chronicles* and *The Song of Roland*. However, in using it I aim rather to invoke Betty Radice's broad view of Classics titles, quoted earlier: whilst many titles may be read as history, as non-fiction, they are all equally works of great literary value.

Before I commence, it is important first to note that I am quite deliberately not going to examine texts that can claim origins in medieval France but are in fact (largely) translations out of Latin, such as *The Letters of Abelard and Heloise*, translated by Betty Radice and first published in 1974, and *The Cistercian World*, a selection of twelfth-century monastic writings published in 1993 and translated by Pauline Matarasso (who will feature here, however, for her medieval French translations for Penguin). The texts that will be covered are Dorothy Sayers's translation of *The Song of Roland*, published in 1957 (reprinted 1965) and the translation of the same text by Glyn S. Burgess in 1990, Geoffrey Brereton's translation of Jean Froissart's *Chronicles* (1968, reprinted 1978), Pauline Matarasso's translations of *The Quest of the Holy Grail* (1969) and *Aucassin and Nicolette and Other Tales* (1971), James Cable's translation of *The Death of King Arthur* (1972), Alan Fedrick's translation of Béroul's *The Romance of Tristan* (1978), Sarah Lawson's translation of Christine de Pizan's *The Treasure of the City of Ladies* (1985, reprinted 2003), Glyn S. Burgess and Keith Busby's translation of *The Lais of Marie de France* (1986, revised 1999) and finally William W. Kibler and Carleton W. Carroll's translation of Chrétien de Troyes's *Arthurian Romances* (1990, revised 2004).[26] The Archive's editorial file designators for each of these titles are to be found in the Bibliography, and it is important to acknowledge that very few, if any, of these files can claim to be complete, though some are more so than others. What I attempt to construct here is therefore based on what I can infer from what remains available. Where possible, I have attempted to fill in gaps via both personal correspondence and interviews with the translators and editors with whom I have been able to make contact; even in those cases, however, an exhaustive analysis was not feasible because they were aware that their memory of events might no longer be perfectly accurate between twenty and sixty years afterwards. Nonetheless, the broad chronological view I take across these titles will enable us to trace developments in the techniques and tactics used by Penguin Classics to bring medieval French to an anglophone audience, and it allow us more insight into Penguin's relationship with the general reader and the academy in the social landscape of post-war Britain, a time of both radical social change and unprecedented technological development.

---

[26] A translation by Rosalind Brown-Grant of Christine de Pizan's *The Book of the City of Ladies* would also appear as a Penguin Classic in 2000, but the Archive does not contain documentation beyond the late 1990s, thus this title has been omitted from this Element.

The first medieval French text to be published by Penguin Classics was *The Song of Roland* (*La Chanson de Roland*), translated by Dorothy Sayers. Sayers (1893–1957) had been an undergraduate student of modern languages at Somerville College, Oxford, but she did not continue into the academic profession, famously becoming a renowned crime fiction writer and poet. The editorial file contains no detail of how Sayers came to take on the role of translator of the *Roland*, nor why Penguin thought this a good text for its list – and I cannot find that Sayers alluded to this elsewhere. However, it is possible to make a couple of educated guesses. In respect of the *Roland* itself, the fact that perhaps the most famous and certainly the oldest surviving manuscript (Oxford, Bodleian Library, MS Digby 23) is in Anglo-Norman and was produced in England tells us much about the importance of the text in England from the Middle Ages onwards, even if it would eventually become something of a national epic in France. The level of the *Roland*'s cultural influence, indeed, is indicated by the international integration and re-imagination of its key motifs, scenes and protagonists in literature across the centuries, from Ariosto's *Orlando furioso* (1516) to Shakespeare's *King Lear* (1608), and from Graham Greene's *The Confidential Agent* (1939) to Stephen King's *The Dark Tower* book series (1998–2004), whose gunslinger protagonist is even called Roland. As a starting point for Penguin's medieval French list, therefore, there were few narratives to rival the *Roland*'s existing profile. As for the choice of Sayers, we know, of course, that Rieu believed that academics were 'enslaved by the idiom of the original language' and thus did not write well (Hare, 2008a, p. 26). His solution was to turn to professional writers who trod a line between scholarly and entertaining; Sayers was in fact amongst the first he courted, and she was ideal, as her existing public profile would help to train the public's eye on Classics (Hare, 2008a, pp. 25–6). Her fine translation for Classics of Dante's *Inferno*, published in 1950, had also enjoyed considerable success; thus, she was a proven asset. Indeed, it seems likely that she was approached for the *Roland* at the behest of Rieu himself. This is supported by a letter from Sayers to her editor, A. S. B. Glover, in which she indicates that her initial discussions for the scope of the book (particularly the inclusion of a couple of illustrations about which Glover had apparently been surprised to hear) had been with Rieu: 'I'm so sorry!'

writes Sayers, 'I told Dr. Rieu all about the proposed illustrations, and he agreed [*sic*], and wrote it all down on the typescript, and I thought you knew all about it' (Sayers to Glover, 28 December 1956).[27] At this point, therefore, Rieu's master plan of creating books for the general reader by using professional writers appears very much still in action. However, the various difficulties of his chosen approach are made explicit in the editorial file's other correspondence.

Sayers, for instance, appears to have had considerable sway in the creative direction of her book and writes to Penguin regularly with ideas, especially regarding design. However, her status as a non-academic led, on occasion, to associated problems. For example, in suggesting designs for the cover roundel, Sayers tells Rieu that Glover's idea of using Roland's horn as a motif is unsuitable (something that Glover later refers to as a 'contemptuous down turn' (Glover to Sayers, 8 November 1956)) and suggests instead to use either a head of Charlemagne or something from the German *Hrodlandslied* as inspiration. A copy, she says, is to be found in the Ashmolean Museum, Oxford (Sayers to Glover, 5 November 1956). This sends Glover on a wild goose chase, since Sayers in fact meant a facsimile edition, and Glover ends up having his knuckles rapped by the slightly testy, if clearly tongue-in-cheek librarian at the Ashmolean, Grace Briggs, who admonishes him for wasting her time: 'I have also been uttering the entirely normal imprecations against an enquirer who provides incomplete, inaccurate or misleading information – or who appears to do so. In short, I cannot find what you want' (Briggs to Glover, 9 November 1956).

Glover takes this on the chin, calling himself 'naughty' (Glover to Briggs, 12 November 1956) and goes back to Sayers for more information. Sayers responds to say that she is in touch with Dr Lewis Thorpe who may have alternative ideas for the roundel; she also provides additional, if still woolly, information on the *Hrodlandslied* facsimile, for she cannot remember the shelf mark, only that it 'is in the Taylorian Library at the Ashmolean, probably catalogued under "Roland" or "Rolandslied" – the

---

[27] All citations from Penguin Archive documents have been transcribed diplomatically, maintaining the original formatting used by the writer in question so as to give as accurate a visual rendering of the documents as possible.

Curator would know' (Sayers to Glover, 14 November 1956). In relaying this to Briggs, Glover refers, clearly jokingly, to Sayers as 'the villain of this particular piece' (Glover to Briggs, 19 November 1956). Briggs writes back saying that, despite efforts, they cannot find anything suitable (Briggs to Glover, 21 November 1956). The matter thus appears to be at an impasse, and Glover laments, 'I will pass on what you say to Dorothy Sayers and insist that she must be more definite in her demands' (Glover to Briggs, 26 November 1956). Fortunately for all concerned, it is the academic mentioned earlier, Lewis Thorpe, who comes to the rescue – he suggests adapting a roundel from the stained glass at Chartres Cathedral that depicts the *Roland* narrative (Sayers to Glover, 10 December 1956). In short, it is the knowledge and precision of an academic that enable matters to move forwards, and this is not the only way in which Thorpe would influence the publication.

Lewis Thorpe was a professor of French at the University of Nottingham from 1958 until his death 1977. He was also president of the International Arthurian Society (1975–7), and would translate five medieval Latin works for Penguin Classics between 1966 and 1978 (his Gerald of Wales was published posthumously). It is difficult to know if Thorpe's role in Sayers's *Roland* was an official one, but he certainly seems to have acted as a kind of academic mentor to Sayers – and not just in respect of cover images. He also appears to have consulted with Sayers on the translation of the text itself. For example, shortly before going to print, Sayers writes to Glover (8 May 1957) confessing that she has made a large number of amendments to the galley proofs. This, she says, is because 'Dr. Lewis Thorpe, who went most carefully over every line of the translation with the O.F. text, felt that I had taken rather too much liberty in reducing so many of the mixed perfects and preterites with which the texts is liberally sprinkled to a uniform historic present.'

Thorpe's academic and linguistic credentials, therefore, seem to be held superior to Sayers's, but why did Thorpe feel the need to intervene, and why did Sayers accept his suggestions? On this matter of style, she states:

> I did this, in the first instance, for the benefit of the general reader – and also with a wary eye on my Editor [Rieu] who

does not, I know, care much for archaic oddities. But,
having seen Dr. Thorpe's point of view, I have come to
agree that one must bear in mind the very considerable
number of university students, who will probably want to
use the translation to assist their French studies, and who
might be misled and bothered. We do not want their tutors
to warn them off the book as being slipshod or incorrect!

Evidently, Sayers had been strongly directed, probably by Rieu, to adopt
a style suitable for the general reader (which apparently consists in simpli-
fying tenses) but is acutely aware – thanks to Thorpe, an academic – that
there is a likely audience for her book amongst university students. Indeed,
in the same letter, she even concerns herself with finding a balance between
these two audiences by suggesting where the textual apparatus should
appear. It should all be 'in one section, so that he [the reader] knows
where to look for it. (The only exception to this is the Note on Ganelon's
Boots, which should be banished to the end of the book for the Academic,
and the Academics only, to quarrel about)'.[28]

What is perhaps most significant is less that Sayers has been made aware
of her academic audience, but that Penguin – represented here by Glover –
seems partially deaf to her numerous suggestions to this end, never once
commenting that she is astute to notice the university market, indeed not
commenting on it at all. Sayers's directions do, nonetheless, seem to have
been carried out, and following a further set of galleys, Sayers declares to

---

[28] Perhaps it is also this tricky balancing act that meant Sayers felt unable to provide
a blurb, having been asked to do so by Penguin. Sayers's rejection of the request
is missing from the file, so we cannot be sure of her reasons, but the fact of it is
evidenced by Glover's response: 'I am sorry for your decision about the blurb,
for after all who can know what a good book yours is so well as yourself, but we
will do our best' (Glover to Sayers, 13 May 1957). A Penguin employee, Pauline
Yettram, steps into the breach: 'I have concocted a blurb from your introduction
to THE SONG OF ROLAND and I should be most grateful if you could let me
know of any alterations you might like to make to it' (Yettram to Sayers,
18 June 1957).

Glover (26 June 1957) that 'Dr. Thorpe thinks it will do!' suggesting – as I alluded to earlier – that Thorpe had assumed an important mentoring role in the translation of this Penguin Classic, and one respected by the publisher. Thus, well before the Robbins Report, the evidence in respect of Sayers's book suggests that whilst Penguin's focus is mostly on the general reader, Sayers's and Thorpe's eyes are trained on the academic market for Classics.

I alluded in Section 2.2 to the fact that Betty Radice would occasionally have new translations of existing Classics done where it was believed that they did not meet the needs of the growing scholarly market. *The Song of Roland* was indeed retranslated by Glyn S. Burgess (published in 1999), but this is far too late to have been part of Radice's programme. Indeed, Penguin seems to have been content with Sayers's book, first reprinting it with a new cover in 1965, and later in 1974, explaining to Derek Rogers, a would-be translator of a new version, that '[i]t seems ... to be a very satisfactory translation and its sales suggest that a great many people think so too. We certainly have no plans at present to replace it with another' (William Sulkin to Rogers, 16 August 1974). Other correspondence in the file also evidences how well Sayers's book was received, and that – for some time – it did manage to strike the balance between scholarly and accessible, since permissions requests to reproduce passages in books come from a range of publishers, including children's publisher J. B. Lippincott (2 February 1966) and Oxford University Press (9 June 1960). That said, a letter from James Cable to Penguin (17 February 1966) that appears in the file for his *The Death of King Arthur* (more about which later) indicates that after a time the academic community became gradually less engaged with it, meaning that an eventual rewrite was almost inevitable. Whilst bewailing the lack of Penguin medieval French translations, Cable says, 'we have only Dorothy Sayers' version of the Song of Roland, which I and many of my colleagues, if I speak frankly, think is pretty awful.'

The internal reasons for Penguin eventually agreeing to a new translation in the late 1980s have, alas, been lost, since the editorial file for Burgess's book is missing from the Penguin Archive. However, Burgess, in a personal email to me from 9 April 2017, recalls: 'It must have been Paul [Keegan] who asked me to replace Dorothy L. Sayers' *Roland* translation, for the very reason that it was too far from the standard English that readers required.' If this is indeed why Penguin moved to replace Sayers's clearly popular book, then it implies that Radice's updates continued well beyond her tenure, and I return to this in Section 3.2. Additional information is found in a letter from Burgess to Paul Keegan (editor of Classics) in the file for *The Lais of Marie de France*, which indicates that Burgess – perhaps feeling similar to Cable about Sayers's translation – may have been the one to propose the *Roland* rewrite: 'I am still hopeful that . . . you will find room for a new <u>Roland</u> which I reckon I could complete in 1988' (11 April 1986). Burgess confirmed to me in an email from 14 November 2018 that he still could not quite remember who approached whom, but that it was entirely possible that he, Burgess, had made the suggestion.

Around the same time that Sayers was preparing her *Roland* manuscript for Penguin, the idea for another medieval French translation had been conceived. On 6 December 1957, Tony Godwin issued a note to the Penguin contracts team to raise a contract with Geoffrey Brereton for a translation of a selection from the *Chronicles* of Jean Froissart with an expected delivery date of 1 August 1959. Brereton (1906–79) had academic credentials, but his main job was as a professional writer and journalist and so seems to have been a Penguin translator in precisely the mould of Rieu's preferred profile. Indeed, the Froissart was not Brereton's first Penguin book, as he had already authored the Pelican Original, *A Short History of French Literature* (1954, second edition 1976) and translated Perrault's *Fairy Tales* (1954). He would also go on to translate several modern French works for Penguin, meaning he – like Sayers – was another known and trusted entity. Despite this, it appears that a bout of ill health prevented Brereton from progressing with his Froissart translation until the early part of 1965, when the correspondence in the file recommences some five and a half years after the original contracted deadline for the manuscript. No documentation has survived that sets out whose initial idea it was to translate Froissart, nor why it was thought to be a suitable text, but there does, by 1965, seem to be some urgency in seeing the long-awaited book through to print.

James Cochrane, then Penguin Classics editor, sends a flurry of chasers to Brereton enquiring after news of the book's progress between February and October of 1965. Brereton seems, from his responses, to be on top of the project, suggesting the end of 1966 as his new final delivery date (Brereton to Cochrane, 20 February 1965). He even asks about the possibility of producing something longer than agreed (Brereton to Cochrane, 26 February 1965), but Cochrane is particularly insistent, especially in his note of 1 October 1965: 'we have been feeling for some time that this is an important gap in the Classics list and we would be reluctant to wait for it any longer.' This urging may well have been prompted by the receipt of a letter to Godwin from Max Reinhardt, who had bought The Bodley Head imprint, in which Reinhardt explains that Graham Greene (one of The Bodley Head's directors) has said: 'there is room now for a good modern translation of Froissart's Chronicles. Lord Berner's is too Elizabethan and antique for our time. There are one or two people who might be able to do the translation, and Graham thought it might be something we could work with you.' This suggests that there was something of a race on to publish the text, that there was a market hungry for the product, perhaps due to broader socio-historic debates that had arisen in the 1960s around the notion of 'feudalism',[29] which would have chimed well with the core themes of Froissart's work. Godwin's response is to inform Reinhardt (20 September 1965) that he is 'in high hopes of receiving his [Brereton's] translation soon', though he does take the opportunity to suggest that Reinhardt might be interested in the hardback rights.

In the spring of 1966, whilst work is progressing on his translation, Brereton writes to Cochrane (29 April 1966) to raise once again the spectre of length, stating that he has already mentioned it to Baldick. Cochrane responds (6 May 1966) to say that he is only aware of an agreement for a longest total length of 175,000 words. Brereton responds quickly (13 May 1966) to clarify: 'I feel convinced that there is a place for a fuller modern translation (the original runs to over a million words) with a rather more substantial critical apparatus. Everyone I have consulted is of the same opinion.' Cochrane therefore writes to the editor of The Penguin Press,

---

[29] Marc Bloch's seminal work of 1939, *Feudal Society*, was first translated into English in 1961, and this led to an almost immediate broadening of the social aspect in medieval historical scholarship so as to include, as a matter of course, all three estates of the realm (clergy, nobility and commoners).

John Knowler, to ask whether the proposal might be suitable for that imprint, stating 'it might have sufficiently large sales in libraries and universities here and in the States to make it worth considering' (18 May 1966). A return memo from Knowler (15 June 1966) is unequivocal: 'The prospect of a Froissart translation more substantial than 175,000 words terrifies me and I think Brereton should be free to take it elsewhere.' Needless to say, Cochrane's response to Brereton (21 June 1966) relates this response in an altogether more tactful manner. However, what this exchange makes very clear is that Penguin's focus is, again, not directly on university markets. Here, even where there is an internal suggestion that such a market might be available, Penguin seems not to feel equipped, or for some reason seems not to wish, to pursue it.

In respect of editorial and cover images, by contrast with Sayers's at times complex wrangling, Brereton appears to have more of a grasp on what would be required. He makes a single cover image suggestion (one from an early printed volume of Froissart), which he has not seen previously reproduced, unlike illuminations from Froissart manuscripts in the British Library, and which would thus distinguish the volume in the market (Brereton to Cochrane, 22 December 1966). Brereton's suggestion is taken up without issue. Similarly, following Brereton's prompt delivery of the manuscript on 30 December 1966, only a very few queries are raised around style, most of which are small scale. Perhaps most relevant is that, as with Sayers, an issue is raised around the use of tenses: 'Robert Baldick mentioned that he was slightly unhappy with the way your linking passages shift between the past tense and the historic present' (Cochrane to Brereton, 28 February 1967). The two men thus agree on a method of making the tenses consistent. This does raise questions as to how integral the use of tenses is to the production of a Penguin translation – it seems, so far at least, to be an area where translators struggle to balance accuracy with readability, which apparently concerns the Classics editors enough to request rewrites of certain sections.

Other than these matters, the route to market of Froissart's *Chronicles* is fairly unremarkable – it was eventually published on 25 April 1968. However, unlike most of the Penguin editorial files that peter out following the associated book's publication, a considerable amount of extant evidence details the Froissart's afterlife, and specifically about the readers who eventually bought and read the volume. On 13 July 1968, for instance, Brereton writes to Cochrane to ask if there had been any other notices of the book other than that in the most recent *Times Saturday Review*. In response, Cochrane confesses:

> As it turns out there does not seem to have been much attention and the reviews of which I am sending you copies are the only ones we can trace. I was particularly irritated to find that in the month in which our Froissart was published the T.L.S. reviewed another and apparently rather bad one and actually said that there was a need for a good modern selection. We responded by sending them another review copy with a covering note.
>
> (Cochrane to Brereton, 17 July 1968)

Cochrane implies that Penguin had sent a previous copy to the *TLS*, but there are signs here that Penguin had not done much market research, with another publisher even beating it to publishing a Froissart translation.[30] Brereton for his part seems to have been an active self-promoter, telling Cochrane (19 July 1968) that he had also written to the *TLS* and found it 'a little unfortunate in the short term that it [the other Froissart] should have appeared only a few months before my Froissart'. In a later note to Cochrane (28 October 1968), he appears hopeful that the favourable review in *TLS* that had by then appeared (thanks, presumably, to Cochrane's

---

[30] This 'other' Froissart was John Joliffe's *Froissart's Chronicles*, published by Harvill in 1967. The *TLS* review that Cochrane mentions was by Malcolm Vale (1968) under the title of 'Medieval Gossip', and it was critical enough to prompt Joliffe (1968) to write a response in the next month's issue. In light of this, it seems particularly ironic that when Penguin started a series gathering together existing classic history works in *c.* 2000 ('Penguin Classic History'), it would select Joliffe's poorly reviewed version of Froissart over Brereton's rather more favourably received one for inclusion in the series (published 2001). Thanks to Samantha Rayner for alerting me to this additional context.

prompt) would boost sales and that he has even 'suggested to the BBC a programme based on the Penguin Froissart'. Brereton thus seems to have been rather savvy about publicity for his volume, and this transpired to be effective.

Good sales followed, for the book was out of print by 1971, as evidenced by a handwritten annotation by someone at Penguin that appears on a letter from Peter Ghosh to Penguin (14 May 1975). Ghosh writes in his capacity as president of the Oxford University History Society to request that the Froissart volume be reprinted, for it is 'quite unobtainable'. Ghosh is not alone in making the request either, since at least two other readers are documented to have appealed to Penguin on this matter (Kenneth Clear, a researcher, 30 January 1976 and Michael Richter, a medieval historian, 14 April 1976). Penguin's response to these requests is to cite poor sales as a reason for not reprinting: 'Its sales record is frankly very disappointing' (William Sulkin to Ghosh, 23 May 1975). Richter, though, points out that he finds this reasoning hard to believe:

> [T]he first edition of this book sold so quickly. In fact, it was sold out before all the scholarly reviews had appeared. This does, after all indicate that there is a substantial market for this book, and I would have thought that the appearance of favourable scholarly reviews would stimulate the demand even more.
>
> (Richter to Penguin, 14 April 1976)

Richter also notes that his desire to see the book reprinted is for his students at Trinity College, Dublin, who 'wish to study original historical documents in translation'. Richter's reasoning as regards supposed poor sales is sound, and Brereton similarly interrogates the matter in a letter from 11 March 1976 to Sulkin. According to Brereton, his royalty accounts record 'total sales of 18,000 for 1968–71 and a further 1,700 until the book disappeared'. He is still convinced, in other words, that there is a market for the book. Even when Sulkin responds to Richter (12 May 1976), he continues the party line that sales 'did in fact tail off quite considerably'. Nonetheless, the repeated appeals do eventually seem to have done the trick, for Sulkin adds: 'However, as it happens, I am at present trying to arrange for the book to be reissued. This depends on our American office ordering a fairly substantial quantity.' The file does not contain details of how the American office responded to Sulkin's enquiry, but one must assume favourably because two years later, on 27 April 1978 (as reported in a note from P. Sadler in Penguin Editorial to Brereton, 24 April 1978), the book was finally reissued.

Yet again, we see here a partial blindness on the side of Penguin to its potential market, despite many prompts from those it could reasonably have trusted to know the available readership. Penguin does not seem to have sent Brereton's book to academic reviewers (or, if it did, such reviews were not chased up in a timely fashion); Penguin did not wish to consider a longer version for an explicitly academic audience, despite the suggestion that a market might exist; Penguin did not note that, even if sales of the book did tail off, the book still went out of print even before any major reviews had appeared, at which point further sales would have been almost assured; even several years and various appeals later, Penguin took a long time to act upon the demands of the academic market that was by then presenting itself so willingly. Indeed, no other Penguin translations of medieval French texts seem to have been explored in the intervening years between the initial approach to Brereton in 1957 and his Froissart's eventual appearance in 1968. However, the late 1960s marked a watershed that gave way to a flurry of activity.

We have seen earlier that as its Classics series gathered steam, Penguin had become increasingly accustomed to receiving offers to translate works. The same would be true of the next two medieval French works to find their way onto Penguin Classics in translations by Pauline Matarasso. Her first undertaking would be *The Quest of the Holy Grail*, a project that she proposed to Penguin, as alluded to in a letter sent to her from James Cochrane, who explains that Baldick has passed on her specimen translation to him, and that they would be pleased to add the text to the Classics list (Cochrane to Matarasso, 9 February 1967). In an interview conducted with Matarasso on 27 October 2017, Matarasso explained to me that she had worked on the translation for her own pleasure to begin with but then started to wonder what to do with it. Classics was, by then, a household name, so she decided to see what Penguin thought. Cochrane's note to Matarasso also indicates that it is, in particular, the US market that has driven their interest in the title, a market to which she had apparently alluded in her proposal. 'As you say, there is' Cochrane says, 'increasing interest in texts of this kind particularly in the USA.'

By contrast with Sayers and Brereton, Matarasso was not a well-known writer, rather a scholar who had approached Penguin with a specimen of her work, as opposed to having been approached by the publisher. The Catalogue Note for Matarasso's title (8 March 1967) contains a short author biography, which describes her as 'Oxford Graduate. Specialist in medieval French literature. Took doctorate in Paris on Raoul de Cambrai'. This is expanded somewhat in the Advance Information Sheet for her *Aucassin and Nicolette* that would follow:

> Pauline Matarasso read modern languages at Lady Margaret Hall, Oxford, and gained First Class Honours in 1950. She was awarded a Doctorat de l'Université de Paris in 1958. Her thesis Recherches historiques et littéroires sur 'Raoul de Cambrai' was published in 1962. She has also translated The Quest of the Holy Grail for Penguin Classics.

Her academic qualifications, then, are apparently important to the marketing of both titles in a way not seen with the previous titles by Sayers and Brereton. Perhaps surprisingly, however, and despite her academic credentials, Matarasso confessed in our interview that she could not remember having had any particular motivation to produce texts for universities – for her, these were personal projects. Did Penguin see it differently, however?

The correspondence in the *Quest*'s editorial file seems to be relatively (though not entirely) complete, while that of *Aucassin and Nicolette* is less so. Both files, however, suggest that Penguin considered Matarasso something of a model translator. Almost no disagreements over style are discussed at any point, for instance. Indeed, the only editorial matter noted is by Matarasso herself in relation to the *Quest*, where she takes issue with an editorial decision to use upper-case letters:

> I still think it is a mistake to use capitals for 'sir', except where the word occurs at the beginning of a sentence. The same would apply to 'Sir Knight'. There seems to me to be no justification for the use of capitals, which is contrary to modern usage and merely gives the printed page a pseudo-archaic look, which I thought was just what 'Classics' wanted to avoid.
>
> (Matarasso to Jennifer Hanrott (Penguin Editorial), 10 July 1969)

On this minor point, she is overruled due to the expense of such an amendment at that moment of production (confirmed in a note from 'Mag' (copy editor) to Hanrott, 19 July 1969), but otherwise the editorial process seems to have been very smooth for both of Matarasso's translations. Even the matter of the cover image seems to have been a relatively relaxed and unproblematic affair, with the cover brief for the *Quest* (10 December 1968) simply stating: 'Something from twelfth or thirteenth century French Arthurian iconography – preferably Galahad or the Grail itself'. There is also a similarly loose instruction in the cover brief for *Aucassin and Nicolette* (18 November 1970): '13th century French miniature depicting courtly life'. Matarasso explained to me in our interview that she could not remember if she had had any hand in suggesting or agreeing to cover images. The file contains a note from her to Frederick Plaat (19 September 1969) about the *Quest*, stating: 'I hope one of your tame experts has found something nice and appropriate for the cover & look forward to seeing it', which seems to confirm that she was not closely involved in the decision-making process. In short, Matarasso appears to have been an easy translator to work with – she was prompt in the delivery of her manuscripts (both were delivered on schedule, and her correspondence with Penguin was regular), and she produced translations that required little editorial intervention. This is evidenced perhaps most clearly by Cochrane's note to Baldick on the receipt of Matarasso's *Quest* manuscript (10 December 1968), which contains a ringing endorsement: 'Just a note to acknowledge receipt of Pauline Matarasso's splendid translation of the Quest of the Holy Grail which I found myself reading from beginning to end for pure pleasure.' Having asked Matarasso during our interview whether Penguin had ever given her instructions or parameters for her translation that might have facilitated her producing something so immediately suitable, she said she could not recall that being the case, and rather wrote as was natural to her. Indeed, the quibble about using upper-case letters even sees her speaking confidently to what she believes Penguin is looking for – an avoidance of pseudo-archaisms.

I suggest it is likely precisely because of the sheer quality of what Matarasso produced, or perhaps we should see it as her natural grasp of what Penguin was seeking (and I will return later to the example that Matarasso's work would come to set) that Penguin Classics was very quick to offer her the contract for *Aucassin and Nicolette*, having done so even before the publication of the *Quest*: 'Robert Baldick has passed on to me your proposal and specimen translation for an edition of Aucassin and Nicolette and I should be very happy to send you a contract for this and for one or two other "contes" that you propose including with it' (Cochrane to Matarasso, 23 June 1969). Again, it should be noted that it is Matarasso who prompts the publication by suggesting a title she is willing to translate. The selection of medieval French texts for publication on Classics, therefore, seems less and less frequently to be driven by Penguin. This is further corroborated by the fact that other would-be translators, as noted earlier, write in abundance to Penguin to suggest titles for publication, some of which are taken up with very little discussion. For example, a PhD student, Richard C. West, wrote to Penguin Books (31 March 1970) to say:

> I am an old and eager reader of medieval works that you publish, but I was more than usually interested by this one [the *Quest*], since I am presently engaged on a similar project [his PhD on medieval literature including the *Quest* and the closely related *Mort Artu*]. I have also been preparing a translation of this Old French romance [the *Mort Artu*] into modern English and it is about this that my dissertation director, Professor Eugene Vinaver, advised me to write to you.

It seems only because another translator has already proposed the same project and had it accepted that West's offer is rejected (Sylvia Cookman to West, 4 May 1970); this other translator is James Cable, to whose translation I return later. Another similar example is provided by Andrew K. Dalby's speculative letter to Penguin (24 May 1971) in the file of *Aucassin and Nicolette*, in which he offers his translation of the same text (which he encloses), only to be told by Anne Scarlett (24 May 1971) that they would have considered the project, but Matarasso's edition was already in press. It is particularly notable for this Element that these requests all come from academics, presumably thinking of their own academic needs, even though Classics was still being outwardly marketed at the general reader. West even states that the impetus for him to write came from an academic supporter: his supervisor, the eminent Arthurian scholar Eugene Vinaver.

In the end, Matarasso's *Quest* in particular sold exceptionally well, spawning reprints in 1971 (Frederick Platt (Managing Editor) to Matarasso, 7 September 1971) and 1975 (Sadler to Matarasso, 20 May 1975).[31] However, Matarasso was amongst the last to know. She only learnt of the first reprint after writing, just a month prior to the publication of *Aucassin and Nicolette*, to enquire after the success of the *Quest* (Matarasso to Plaat, 5 September 1971). It is only with the response (which comes directly from Platt since Cochrane was currently on leave) that she hears the news:

> I am sorry to hear that you are at the receiving end of some of the alienating effects which a firm of our size has to engender! However, I hasten to answer at least one question in your letter: THE QUEST OF THE HOLY GRAIL has just reprinted. ... Don't apologize for troubling me, my heart goes out to people who try to communicate with this sometimes seemingly headless leviathan.
> (Plaat to Matarasso, 7 September 1971)

---

[31] Equivalent sales information for *Aucassin and Nicolette* is not to be found in the file, unfortunately.

Plaat's strikingly honest response here suggests that Penguin may have become a victim of its own success and was by now unable to keep up regular correspondence with all of its authors. Indeed, Cochrane follows up on his return from leave:

> The trouble is that we have grown to be a very large organisation, we publish a very large number of books every year, and it isn't possible to keep in touch with all our authors and translators as closely as we should all like. We originally printed 15,000 copies of The Quest of the Holy Grail, and as you know it is being reprinted this month. Of those 15,000 copies, approximately 3,000 have been sold in the United States. No reviews were sent to us by our presscuttings service, and I'm a little disturbed that you should have heard of reviews in the Irish press, copies of which should certainly have been sent to us.
> (Cochrane to Matarasso, 4 October 1971)

The communications issue thus seems to extend not only to corresponding with authors but also to keeping a firm hand on publicity (an issue that we also witnessed with Brereton's translation of Froissart), thus giving an impression that Penguin's commercial success with Classics may have had less to do with advance planning, and more with luck of timing.

A similarly haphazard route to contract is also true of Alan Fedrick's translation of Béroul's *Tristan*, published in May 1970. The editorial file for this title is comparatively slim, but it does contain evidence that, once again, it was Fedrick (1937–75) – an academic in French at Royal Holloway, and latterly at Brandeis University, Massachusetts – who approached Penguin, and not vice versa. He suggests Béroul's text to Penguin because it is 'frequently prescribed for study in the majority of English (and indeed American) Universities, and no translation into English at present exists' (Fedrick to Penguin Books, 15 September 1967). Cochrane quickly refers Fedrick's specimen to Baldick for approval (6 October 1967). Perhaps because of Fedrick's very clear designation of the text as one aimed at students, Cochrane – rather uncharacteristically – even asks for Baldick's thoughts on 'how important [the text is] in French literature courses around the Universities, etc, etc: I must say I have some doubts about taking on another Tristan for purely commercial reasons'.[32] Indeed, even the Catalogue Note for the eventual title reproduces Fedrick's academic rationale for publication almost word-for-word. Whilst there is no memo from Baldick in response to Cochrane in the file, presumably he answered favourably since Cochrane confirms Penguin's interest in a letter to Fedrick on 19 January 1968 and requests a specimen. Fedrick duly obliges and the book is agreed for contract by the end of the month (Cochrane to Fedrick, 30 January 1968), with the advice that Fedrick should contact Baldick to discuss the translation before setting down to work. As with Matarasso, then, Fedrick's proposal is unsolicited, and yet Penguin is remarkably quick to act on it. The editorial files, in other words, suggest a reactive list strategy, one that evidences Penguin to have been skilled at grasping opportunities as they arose, rather than seeking them out proactively.

Fedrick responds gratefully to Cochrane (31 January 1968) and astutely asks: 'May I ask whether the book will be for sale in the U.S.A. and Canada?' Cochrane answers that it will be, and that Penguin expects 'it will do particularly well since there is a heavy demand around the collages [*sic*] for texts in medieval French' (2 February 1968). It is quite unusual here to see Cochrane open to the idea of this book as one for universities, though again, his particular slant is on the US market, just as it had been with Matarasso. Also similar to Matarasso, the cover brief (22 April 1969) is relatively loose but contains one precise suggestion which indicates that Fedrick may actually have had some input: 'Anything from the wide variety of medieval treatments of the theme, but see especially the picture of Mark finding the lovers in the forest in R.S. Loomis: Arthurian Literature in the Middle Ages.' As far as the file documents, then, the route to press of *Tristan* was unproblematic. There is no mention of major style revisions or significant delays to production, and the book was published in May 1970.

---

[32] Classics had already published A. T. Hatto's translation of Gottfried von Strassburg's *Tristan* in 1970.

Its commercial success is indicated by its reprinting in 1978, though this publication was posthumous, as Fedrick died in 1975.

Fedrick thus enjoyed a fairly straightforward experience with his medieval French Classic, and one wonders if he ever discussed it with his colleague in French at Royal Holloway, James Cable. Cable would produce another medieval French Classic, *The Death of King Arthur* (a translation of the Vulgate Cycle's *La Mort le Roi Artu*), eventually published in November 1971, just one month after Matarassso's *Aucassin and Nicolette*. Cable's experience with Penguin carried some of the same hallmarks but gave rise to rather more complications than did the books of Matarasso and Fedrick. The editorial file attests that the initial conception of Cable's project was inspired as early as 17 February 1966, when Cable writes to the editors of Penguin Classics to say:

> As a University lecturer in French, and as a specialist of the Medieval Period in particular, I have often regretted that your excellent Penguin Classics series contains very few translations from Old French. ... In fact very few translations of 12th and 13th century French literature exist at all in Modern English, although this is certainly not because worthwhile works do not exist. I am thinking for example of the Arthurian romances of Chrétien de Troyes, or the Roman de la Rose, the Roman de Renart or even the 13th cent. prose version of the Queste del Saint Graal, all of which could appeal to modern readers. Would I be expecting too much if I expressed a hope that you might be considering adding even one of these to your collection?

A month or so later, on 10 March 1966, Cochrane responds:

> Your suggestion that we include more works from Medieval French in this series is certainly an interesting one and I should be glad to consider this further and discuss it with our Classics advisor. Do I take it from you [*sic*] letter that you propose to translate one or other of these works yourself?

As elsewhere, then, it is a mere chance enquiry from an academic (Cable was lecturer of French, though he would later leave the academy to work in computing) as to the availability of texts on Classics – not even an actual proposal to translate – that leads Penguin to consider developing its medieval French list. Again, therefore, Penguin seems to grasp an opportunity that presents itself, rather than operating according to a proactive strategy as such.

The suggestion obviously required considerable thought, for Cable only responds to Cochrane some seventeen months later on 2 July 1967: 'after lecturing on the early 13th cent. Prose La Mort le Roi Artu, I have for some time been considering attempting a translation of this fine work, which as far as I know has never been published in English.' Cochrane requests a specimen and synopsis (10 October 1967), which Cable duly provides (6 November 1967), and Cochrane, via his secretary, says he will consult with Baldick ('our advisor') and Penguin's representatives in the United States (Joanna Hordern to Cable, 13 November 1967). In a letter to Christopher Dolley, head of the Penguin US operation, Cochrane seems underwhelmed by the title: 'I'm entirely neutral about works of this kind, which I imagine might have a better chance with you than over here. If you thought you might do well with it I'd be glad to take it further' (13 November 1967). This letter evidences once again the sway that the US market could have in moving a medieval French title to press. Fortunately for Cable, Dolley appears to have a developed sense of the appeal of these books. As Dolley explains to Cochrane,

> [T]here is a growing demand for medieval material, particularly in the Romance Languages, and I would be prepared to give you a respectable order of 6/8000 copies. It seems a book which is of the kind to stimulate jaded students in English and World Literature courses. Poisoned apples and chastity belts are a salable combination!
> (28 November 1967)

By the late 1960s, then, the evidence we have seen here supports my hypothesis in Section 2 that Penguin Classics seems not to have appreciated the fast-growing UK student population that followed the Robbins Report as a potential core market (Hare, 1995, p. 189), even though Penguin US, which was experiencing a similar higher education phenomenon, did. As with the other titles discussed, indeed, the burgeoning UK student market seems only to draw the attention of the academic associated with the title, as is shown when, in filling out the Publicity Information Sheet for his book, Cable cites two main markets: first, '[u]niversity students who have to study work as set text' and second, '[g]eneral public interested in Arthurian tales, & wishing to find a different viewpoint from Malory's'. In spite of Cable's clear identification of the student market (cleverly balanced alongside, though prioritised over, Penguin's more favoured general reader), it is only once Dolley sends his offer to purchase six thousand to eight thousand copies for the United States that Cochrane writes to Cable (19 January 1968) to offer him a contract. In this same letter, we also see a further similarity to Fedrick's experience, whereby Cochrane suggests that it would be sensible for Cable to discuss his translation with Baldick. Again, he does not say why, though later correspondence in the file suggests it was to gain editorial guidance for producing the text.

We have, of course, seen glimpses in the cases of other titles of the question as to what constituted an appropriate editorial style for a Penguin Classic. In the cases of Sayers and Brereton, the matter of tenses proved to be a tricky area, but nowhere have I found a circumscribed set of parameters, or notes of guidance, for translators (cf. Crowe, 2012). Famously, of course, E. V. Rieu's directive was simply that translators should 'Write English' (Hare, 1995, p. 187). This is, though, vague at best, even if taken in the spirit it was clearly intended: that the text should be accessible and enjoyable for a general readership. Williams (1956, p. 19) attempts to define Rieu's mantra more precisely as being to present the text 'in contemporary English without any transgressions of scholarship or textual accuracy'; as we have seen, though, such transgressions – particularly in respect of accuracy – do end up dogging the translators who are conscious of their student readers. Perhaps a more accurate interpretation is Hare's (1995, p. 188), which states that Rieu strove for a 'principle of equivalent effect … a certain quality in the translation capable of creating the same impression on modern-day readers as the original had on its contemporaries'. Even still, whilst *what* a translator is meant to achieve is relatively clear, it is less obvious precisely *how* to achieve it.

It might be, of course, that some authors received informal (or even formal) mentoring, as is implied by Cochrane's invitations to both Cable and Fedrick to discuss their translations with Baldick, though it will be remembered that Matarasso did not recall any such interactions. Cable also seems not to have received such advice, even in spite of Cochrane's suggestion, as he would fall foul of what it was that Penguin sought. After Cable submitted his manuscript on 29 May 1969, a series of letters between Cable and Cochrane address the fact that Baldick, having read the manuscript, had requested that Cable 'revise the style in order to bring it into line with The Quest of the Holy Grail' (Cable to Cochrane, 19 August 1969). Cable expresses his frustration in the same letter:

> I do not feel inclined to put in any extra work on my translation. I am fully satisfied with it as it stands; it is my translation, written in my style of translating Old French texts. ... I was given no guidance beforehand on any editorial principles that might exist. ... You commissioned my translation after receiving a specimen in which the characteristics of my style were apparent. Before beginning the main part of the work, I wrote to Dr Baldick asking him if he had any general advice or instructions to give me. I never received a response to my letter.

After a back-and-forth exchange, Cochrane eventually responds to say:

> That our translations should 'read like a modern novel' is still in a general sense our policy, but it seems to me that your attempt to render a medieval French text into modern colloquial English is not wholly successful and that, in particular, the use of abbreviated forms such as 'you'll' in a context which is in other respects so very remote from us sounds if anything slightly more odd and 'archaic' than a simple and direct style such as Mrs Matarasso has used for her translation of The Quest of the Holy Grail.
> (Cochrane to Cable, 3 October 1969)

What is important here is that rather than archaisms effecting a stylistic issue (which caused the large number of corrections to Sayers's galley proofs, and which worried Matarasso in respect of the use of an upper-case 's' for 'Sir'), it is in fact modern style – specifically contractions – that seems to be problematic for Cable. Using such contractions is apparently too modern for a setting that is 'remote'. As alluded to earlier, too, we see Matarasso's style held up as a particular example for Cable to follow, and if Cable does not make the required amendments, Cochrane says that Penguin will not publish the translation. A further familiar scenario is also alluded to with the reference to communication problems at Penguin (as experienced by Matarasso), whereby Cable's letter to Baldick asking for guidance went unanswered.[33]

Clearly exasperated, Cable responds (6 October 1969) and agrees to 'forgo the contractions that you dislike' and laments:

> I'm afraid I'm just not clever enough to adapt my style to Mrs Matarasso's, or anyone else's. All I can say is that if your concern for an identity of style between the two translations is so great, you should either 1) have commissioned the same person to do the two translations, or 2) be prepared to carry out any necessary editorial synthesis yourselves, or 3) have provided me with suitable guidance at a time when I was still planning my translation. . . . Even now I have no clear idea of the exact points to which you take exception.

Cochrane's response to Cable is not in the file, but a note from Cochrane to Baldick about the matter (15 October 1969) states: 'My feeling is that if Cable starts working through the typescript again to remove the "isn'ts" and "you'lls" he will if he has any sensitivity start noticing other mannerisms that don't work either.' Whatever Cochrane's eventual letter to Cable stated, Cable worked quickly to revise the first forty pages, 'suppressing <u>all</u>

---

[33] Fedrick's file contains no evidence of whether Baldick ever responded to Fedrick's request to meet in Oxford to discuss the translation, which Fedrick indicated to Cochrane he would send (31 January 1968).

the contractions, and making certain other changes', so as to obtain
Baldick's approval before proceeding further (Cable to Cochrane, 1
November 1969). Following this is a hiatus in correspondence in the file,
and the final, accepted manuscript is not recorded as delivered until a year
later in November 1970 (evidenced by the title's undated 'Editorial 1–2' and
a note from Cochrane to Doug Rust (24 November 1970) asking for the
Cable's manuscript delivery payment to be made); the book was finally
published in November 1971. Perhaps Cable fell ill, or maybe the required
revisions were rather more involved than just removing contractions after
all. The latter seems – at first glance – unlikely, since Cochrane's note to
Baldick indicates he believes the exercise is fairly simple and, in an earlier
letter to Cable, he even called the required adjustments 'quite slight'
(3 October 1969). If it really was a simple set of revisions – something
that a qualified copy editor could have implemented with ease – then it
seems odd that it should stand between the manuscript and its publication.
Perhaps, then, Penguin's lack of clarity as to its own style policies was not
just something that confused translators, but also its own staff; perhaps
precisely because they could not identify and articulate the nuts and bolts of
Penguin's style, they were equally ill adept at quantifying how much work
would be required to achieve the desired product.

Cable's was the last medieval French translation of the 1970s, and almost
without exception, all titles up to that point can claim several similarities.
The notion of what constituted a good Penguin Classic translation was
blurred – some translators grasped it immediately, some did not, but it
seems the editors at Penguin could not articulate precisely what they wanted
either. Furthermore, Penguin seems to have become overwhelmed by its
own success, and its communications (or lack thereof) caused issues and
frustrations amongst its translators. Perhaps most importantly, academics
promoted all titles in one way or another – even Sayers's through the
involvement of Thorpe – though some translators were clearly more firmly
focused than others on the university market for their work – in particular,
and perhaps unsurprisingly, those holding academic posts. Even where such
UK markets were firmly pointed out to Penguin by the translators, however, it only appeared to take notice of the US university expansion, where
'after ten years half of Baltimore [the Penguin US office location] turnover

was made up of orders explicitly for school or college syllabuses and that most of these were purchased as classroom-texts' (Morpurgo, 1979, p. 249). By contrast, and despite operating in a similar climate of expanding higher education, Penguin UK kept the fabled general reader at the centre of its focus. J. E. Morpurgo (1979, p. 244), Allen Lane's biographer, supports this with his suggestion that Lane's leadership underpinned why Penguin and Classics seemed reluctant to pursue a more university-focused strategy:

> Bemused by the Penguin legend of service to the individual reader, Allen and his Harmondsworth advisers saw all this [the university market] as a convenient addition to the number of those blessed by their educational preparation with the will to invade bookshops in the quest for Penguins. Because he was short on understanding pedagogic processes Allen failed to grasp that British and American educational methods were converging; like their American equivalents, British schools and universities were coming to use Penguins in large numbers as text books ... the spectacular prospect of large sales created by the will of schools and universities to use Penguins as classroom-texts was seen only dimly from Harmondsworth even some years after the practice had become commonplace. Only then was applicability to academic use (almost from the beginning an incidental but unspoken Penguin tenet) made explicit in editorial and sales policy.

This suggests that Penguin would eventually come to understand its market better, and by extension also how to articulate the nature of its product in terms of style. A new wave of Classics would arrive from the early 1980s onwards. In the next section, I propose to consider those medieval French titles published after 1980 – a time of rapid development in communications and information technologies (not least the advent of the Internet in the 1990s) that would affect both reading and publishing practices and bring about related sociocultural change – to see if Penguin Classics did in fact develop a better grasp of this university audience by that time, particularly in the United Kingdom.

3.2 Relaunch: 1980–1999

Penguin relaunched Classics in 1985, a major part of which was, thanks to the arrival of a new art director, Steve Kent (Baines, 2005, p. 165), a redesign of the cover template. The new style consisted of a light-coloured background with a black spine and a colour-coded mark to indicate the language and period of the text (Yates, 2008, pp. 33–4), and the US arm of Penguin was closely involved in the decision.[34] Indeed, the US market's importance had become so great by this time that 'any big decisions regarding the Classics list had to be taken in conjunction with the US arm of the company, as they represented a sizeable part of Penguin's worldwide Classics market' (Baines, 2005, p. 223). It is perhaps not surprising, therefore, that we have seen increasing references to the US market in the files of the titles explored earlier, as well as that specific consultation of the US office was required before agreeing to projects. The first medieval French text to appear on Classics with the new branding was Christine de Pizan's *The Treasure of the City of Ladies*, translated by Sarah Lawson and published in 1985. Unfortunately, this is amongst the slimmest of all the editorial files to which I have had access, but it nonetheless tells us something of the story of this text's route to press and offers an insight into just how buoyant the US market really was.

The associated correspondence predates considerably the Classics rebrand, with the earliest document being a letter from Sarah Lawson herself. Writing to Donald McFarlan, editor of Classics (16 June 1982), she proposes the translation, upon which she has already commenced work: 'I am translating a work from Middle French, and I think it might fit into your list of medieval classics.' She goes on to provide a short synopsis and notes that she had previously approached Virago due to the narrative's feminist angle, but Virago believed the text was too old, even though

---

[34] Such negotiations were often 'a long and bloody process' according to Kathryn Court, publisher at Penguin, speaking of her experience with the 2003 Classics rebrand (quoted in Buckley, 2010, p. 190).

'Christine de Pizan was the first European woman to earn her living by writing and was, for her time, a daring feminist.' Lawson makes no mention of the scholarly market, but she had a PhD and went on to become a professional writer. A handwritten note at the bottom of the letter in an anonymous hand (possibly McFarlan's since it is he to whom the letter is addressed) simply states: 'we're interested.' A Penguin representative (anonymous thanks to a printing error) responds on 4 August 1982 to ask for specimen chapters. Unfortunately, there is no other correspondence thereafter until 21 February 1983 when Lawson writes to McFarlan to return the contract with a series of amendments. The handwritten notes on this letter, initialled by McFarlan, indicate that Lawson's requests were met. A further postcard from 17 March 1983, by which time the amended contract had been signed and countersigned, sees Lawson request of McFarlan to make a further (somewhat curious) amendment to the contract:

> [E]verything seems to be in order except paragraph 16. Christine would have been very interested in the idea of copyright had it existed in 1400, but now, dead these 550 years, she would have little use for it. It would no sooner be proclaimed than it would lapse rather decisively.

Lawson also notes that she is 'still making enquiries at the British Library about a Christine exhibition'. This is unfortunately all of the documentary evidence available in respect of this title. Even so, we can still recognise a number of similarities with our other titles: a translator with academic credentials approaches Penguin to propose a title rather than the other way around and that translator makes their own efforts in respect of publicity, as would be more typical when working with an academic press rather than a trade one. Even by the 1980s, then, and following a tactical relaunch of Classics, Penguin's success still seems to have relied upon a reactive rather than proactive approach.

As alluded to earlier, the same file also contains an unexpected insight into the burgeoning US market for medieval French. I say unexpected since the letter in question seems to have been misfiled: it is not to do with Lawson's translation. Dated 22 July 1982, it comes from Karen Braziller, associate publisher at Persea Books, and is addressed to Sally Gaminara at Penguin. Braziller has discussed another work by Christine de Pizan, *The Book of the City of Ladies*, over the phone with Gaminara. Persea had recently published this in hardback and it had been successful: 'The book is actually cresting some waves here. It is displaying in all bookstores face out, and is reordering like mad.' She recounts that it has also had media coverage from, amongst others, *Vogue*, the *Washington Post*, the *New York Times* and even on radio programmes. Braziller notes:

> Penguin U.S. (Gerry Howard) had made us an early, small-ish offer which included English publication as a Penguin Classic. We turned him down, but I wonder if, in view of the enclosed reviews and the attention the book is receiving here, you would reconsider it for Allen Lane/Penguin or just for Penguin?

This work by Christine de Pizan would not become a Penguin Classic until 2000, when it was translated by UK academic Rosalind Brown-Grant (unfortunately, the associated editorial file is missing). This publication, though, confirms that Persea's offer was not taken up. Knowing why, however, is more difficult. A handwritten note on the letter from Persea states: 'World Rights in Two Years time? Costs – RK'. This indicates that the proposal was given consideration, but one wonders if confusion was caused by the fact that, only one month beforehand, Lawson had submitted a proposal in respect of a different Christine de Pizan text, but one with a very similar title. Did Penguin misconstrue it as the same work? Given that the letter from Persea appears in the Lawson file, this is not impossible. Indeed, even Lawson herself, in her initial proposal letter, warns Penguin that the two texts are often confused. Once again, then, there is evidence that Penguin UK's focus had shifted firmly to the US market by this time, and that it is still less well versed in the particulars of its medieval French titles.

Penguin's subsequent medieval French Classic *The Lais of Marie de France*, translated by Glyn S. Burgess (University of Liverpool) and Keith Busby (then Utrecht University) and published in 1986, also has a similarly small editorial file – a symptom, perhaps, of a world now moving away from letter writing and increasingly towards telephony as a form of correspondence thanks to technological advancement. No evidence remains for how Penguin came to commission the project, but Busby (in person) and Burgess (in an email of 7 April 2017) explained to me that they discovered at a British Branch meeting of the International Courtly Literature Society that they were each working on Marie de France projects. They decided to propose a joint translation project to Betty Radice, particularly because they wanted to provide an edition for students that would replace that already published in Everyman. Burgess reports in the same email that Radice

> liked the translation but that, after discussions with some Penguin staff members, it was felt that it was too literal. So, . . . initially it was 'rebuffed'. I cannot remember whether in her letter of rejection Betty asked us to re-submit or whether it was some time later that she wrote and asked me to revise one of the lays and send it to her. Whenever it was, I did this and sent her *Guigemar*, as a result of which she invited me to come down from Liverpool to meet with her in London. At our meeting she said how much she liked the new version (all I had done was to add a few conjunctions and get rid of short sentences!) and that Penguin was now willing to offer us a contract if we would revise all the lays to make them more readable for the general public.

Several of the now familiar characteristics are once again in evidence here: the project is proposed by academics for a university market, while Penguin's eye is still clearly on the general reader; at the same time a tricky-to-articulate style issue – one with, in the end, a straightforward solution – prevents the work from progressing. Burgess added in his email to me: 'there was never any specific recommendation about style' except that 'they had a distinct dislike of footnotes, for which I have a great predilection.' A letter in the file from Burgess to Keegan (30 March 1985) corroborates that Burgess and Busby did not feel entirely confident that they had met with Penguin's expectations, even after the manuscript's delivery:

> I spoke on the telephone yesterday to my collaborator Keith Busby, who asked me to request of you that if our text is submitted to an outside reader this be done anonymously. Our text has, of course, had the advantage of being read by Betty Radice who made some valuable comments and it has been prepared by two translators. So each part of it has already been checked for accuracy by another reader. A careful reading for purposes of style could perhaps be done within Penguin Books, as you must have many experts in this area.

Still, then, there is an impression of translators who are not entirely sure what is being asked of them thanks to Penguin's failure to describe its editorial policy clearly. Penguin's attempt, furthermore, is still to satisfy the general reader whilst its translators strive for products suitable for academic settings. In respect of the target audience, further confirmation of Penguin's focus on the US market is provided by Burgess's email of 7 April 2017, where he notes that he had been made aware 'that the UK side of Penguin could not make decisions about new titles. Decisions were made by the US side'.

The eventual success of the *Lais* is suggested not only by the fact that it was reissued in 1999 with two extra lays in Old French but also by Burgess's email (7 April 2017) in which he recalls that Radice had indicated he and Busby should expect only modest sales, and that a print run of around 7000 was likely. The Publishing Brief (19 July 1984) in the file indeed estimates a modest run, albeit a little higher: 10,000 with a domestic sales estimate of 3000. Being in regular receipt of royalty statements, Burgess was able to offer some figures of actual sales:

> I used to keep precise figures, but stopped when the total reached around 110,000! That was quite a few years ago, so I estimate it at around 160,000 now (it sold 2,500 copies in the last six months, which is quite pleasing for a book that is over thirty years old).

As well as proposing to translate other medieval French titles for Penguin, Burgess seems also to have had a hand in the final title that I will consider here: *Arthurian Romances*, a translation of the works of Chrétien de Troyes by William W. Kibler (with the exception of *Erec and Enide*, which was translated by Carleton W. Carroll). Amongst the first evidence of this title's conception is a letter in the *Lais* file, in which Burgess explains to Keegan: 'I have just received Professor Kibler's translation of Yvain for review in Speculum. I'll let you know eventually whether it would make a good volume in Penguin Classics' (11 April 1986). This suggests that Penguin had sought Burgess's advice in respect of publishing at least one of Chrétien de Troyes's romances. Indeed, Penguin appears to have been trying to publish Chrétien's works for many years, as is evidenced by a Cancellation of Contract note dated 31 August 1988 in the *Arthurian Romances* file – however, this is not for Kibler's translation. Instead, this cancellation note relates to a much earlier contract for a translation of Chrétien's *Lancelot*. The reason for cancellation states: 'Non-delivery of MS (20 years late!)' This indicates that, remarkably, Chrétien had been in Penguin's sights since at least 1968, or perhaps even earlier, though whether the idea had come from Penguin or from outside (as has been the case with our other titles) is difficult to know.

One piece of evidence suggests that even if the Chrétien idea had originally been an external one, Penguin at least took it seriously enough to approach various translators to tackle the project, as shown by a letter from Matarasso to Cochrane (1 June 1972) in the *Quest* file. Matarasso states:

> Dr Baldick rang me up some eighteen months ago or maybe less about a proposal to translate this text. I said then and still think that of all Chrétien's romances it is the least suitable to offer that mythical personage, the General Reader, in that it is unfinished and there is nothing more irritating than an unfinished work. What is even worse is that its meaning is so enigmatic that scholars still argue annually about the import of the key passages. However perhaps your readers will lap it up as a literary conundrum. And obviously if you are embarking on the complete canon then it cannot be left out.

The text to which Matarasso refers is, surely, the *Conte du Graal* (Story of the Grail), the famously unfinished final romance authored by Chrétien before, it is believed, he died, possibly even pen-in-hand. The text's very incompleteness, she believes, would not appeal to Penguin's favoured audience, the general reader. Given the large and still expanding body of scholarship on this narrative, too, with hindsight, it seems naïve of Matarasso to think that the narrative's mystery would be off-putting rather than alluring. What is particularly important here is that even though the Cancellation of Contract note pertained to a translation only of *Lancelot*, Matarasso's phrase 'the complete canon' evidences beyond reasonable doubt that it was in fact the publication of all of Chrétien's romances that had been considered as early as the late 1960s. Given the more than twenty-year hiatus between concept and eventual product, Chrétien's romances, we might say, presented as many problems in respect of 'unfinishedness' in the 1960s and 1970s as they had in the twelfth century.

The earliest document in the editorial file for *Arthurian Romances* itself, which gives more information on the revisiting of the Chrétien initiative in the 1980s, is a letter from Burgess to Keegan (2 February 1986), where the reason for Burgess's mention of Kibler's *Yvain* in the earlier cited letter from the *Lais* file is revealed. Burgess is fulfilling a request to review a translation of *Yvain* by Burton Raffel, which Penguin had been considering for publication. Burgess believed that Raffel's version was too free for the style of the Classics series, since, as he said, 'Penguin Books are heavily used by students'; to Burgess, close and accurate translation was an indispensable characteristic of a Classic, something that, according to his email of 9 April 2017, he still stands by: 'I feel that anyone using a Penguin Classics translation is likely to want a readable but accurate rendering of the text.' Despite this leading to Penguin's rejection of Raffel's manuscript, the translation eventually appeared with the University of California Press in 1987, and that book will claim an additional significance later. To return to Burgess's letter to Keegan, though, we find Burgess keen to assist in a project of this nature, even if Raffel's particular rendering is not to be the vehicle. Burgess expresses an urgent need amongst students of Old French and Middle English for an affordable edition of all of Chrétien's works, pointing out that those published by the likes of Garland, the

University of Georgia Press and Everyman were 'outside the reach of students'. He also explains that he has recently reviewed Kibler's facing translation of *Lancelot* in the Garland series for *Romance Philology*. 'This was excellent', he says 'and in [Kibler's] case we are dealing with a genuine Old French scholar'. Burgess adds: '[Kibler] will shortly be writing to you to suggest a prose version of all the Chrétien romances.' So Burgess, the translator of an existing Penguin medieval French title and an academic, turns out to be a key driver in inspiring not only the scope of the proposed publication (that one volume should contain all romances, rather than having each one individually translated and published) but also the selection of a translator. He is also transparent in his vision of the publication as being meant for an academic setting, and thus that the text should be academically rigorous.

Sure enough, albeit some months later, Kibler eventually writes to Keegan (22 August 1986), '[a]t the urging of Professor Glyn Burgess' to express an interest in undertaking the Chrétien project. He explains that Garland has agreed to relinquish its rights to the English translations of Chrétien's works that he has so far produced and states that he would be willing to extract these from the existing facing edition and prepare them for publication in a single-language edition for Penguin. In a later letter to Keegan (22 January 1987), Kibler adds that he has not yet tackled either Chrétien's *Cligés* (which he plans to do) or *Erec and Enide*, but that Carroll had produced a facing translation of the latter for Garland in the same series as his own, which could be suitable for inclusion in the Penguin edition, especially as this would save the time and effort of Kibler starting from scratch and thus enable an earlier delivery date for the manuscript. With this in mind, he had taken the liberty of additionally acquiring approval in principle from Garland for the use of the English translation of *Erec*. Given the trials of getting a 'Penguin Chrétien' published that resulted in an interval of twenty years, the route to press is actually fairly unremarkable after this point. With just a few delays caused by (once again) communication issues about contracts on Penguin's side, Kibler and Carroll delivered their manuscript in late 1989 and the title was published in January 1991. An internal memo from Keegan to Kate McFarlan (22 February 1990) alerts us once again to the perceived importance of the US market, where he urges publication by no later than January or February 1991 'given the interest expressed by Penguin US'. This title, too, appears not to have escaped the style question raised in respect of almost every other translation considered here. Upon delivery of the manuscript, for instance, Kibler requests that Keegan inform him as to 'what stylistic changes are introduced' (6 July 1989). Kibler receives an assurance shortly afterwards (31 July 1989), which explains that 'copy-editorial will Penguinize the text'. This is the first time that this term appears in any of the files studied in this book, but it is found in other documentary sources.

The term 'Penguinize' is used, for instance, by Williams (1956, p. 47): 'Novelists are in favour of Penguinizing some of their books; it gets them a wider circle of interest and attention. ... The economic advantages of Penguinization are convincing to all', as well as in a similar context in Penguin's golden anniversary volume (Penguin Books, 1960, p. 36): 'and we ourselves, from our own knowledge of books and from our experience of our readers' tastes and desires, add our quota to the endless flow of candidates for Penguinization.' These two examples seem to suggest something broader than that alluded to by Keegan: specifically, the entire process and effect of publishing a book with Penguin. Charles Clark (commissioning editor at Penguin) offers a tighter definition when writing to David Daiches (editor of the Penguin English Library) about Pelicans, where a variation on the same formula is used:

> The 'Pelicanization' of expert knowledge about the novels in the form of authoritative texts, intros and notes will be our main weapon in selling the very large quantity that we have to see to get the pricing anywhere near competitive with other series. And Pelicanization means the will and ability to get expert knowledge over (and the feeling that such knowledge is relevant to the layman) without either pedantry or talking down.
>
> (Quoted in Donaldson, 2013, p. 122)

Here, the formula indicates a still broad objective, which is to make a text accessible for the general reader, but with only limited specifics as to what that entails. Keegan's letter to Kibler (31 July 1989), by contrast, seems to apply the term more specifically to up-close editorial work, boiling it down to something less complex: 'i.e. adopt a fairly straightforward policy regarding matters of spelling'. Can 'Penguinization' really be just a matter of orthography? One suggestion that this cannot be true is provided when Kibler and Carroll make amendments to the blurb proposed by Penguin for their book, amongst which is the idea to describe *Yvain* as 'a tale of love won, lost, and won again'. Kibler, apparently unsure at whom he is pitching the blurb, asks 'Or is that too popular romance or soap opera?' (Kibler to Keegan, 23 August 1989). A handwritten note on the letter, dated 13 October 1989, states 'Sue M says she prefers to use her version.' Here, then, the matter at hand seems to be register and style. We have also seen elsewhere that 'Penguinization', even if not referred to as such, could entail anything from the removal of archaisms and contractions to the amendment of tenses. In other words, Penguin's articulation of its regime of 'Penguinization', which in the case of *Arthurian Romances* transpires also to entail stylistic considerations and not just spelling as Keegan had suggested, lacks specificity. Even in spite of having 'a term of reference' (Penguinization), which would imply a circumscribed definition, translators remain unsure as to the position of the line between colloquial and academic.

Such haziness, as we have seen with other titles, also extends to matters of cover design. Even though from 1985 there was a new high-end template for Classics covers, the consideration of which cover image would best sell *Arthurian Romances* was relaxed by comparison. The loose cover briefs we saw earlier are matched here by Keegan's hesitant briefing of the designer, Josine Meijer, in respect of which image to use. Keegan's memo to Meijer (16 March 1989) states that Kibler has requested 'a miniature from the Princeton Garrett manuscript 125 of Chrétien's Romances – I think', he says, clearly unsure, 'this refers to a manuscript in Princeton University'. When Kibler writes to inform Keegan (6 July 1989) that, unfortunately, the very same manuscript image has been used for the cover of Burton Raffel's by now recently published translation of *Yvain* for the University of California Press, Keegan's response simply states, 'It does not matter' (31 July 1989). Even putting aside the odd disregard for the principle of distinguishing your product visually in the marketplace, the fact that Raffel's translation was the same that had been rejected by Penguin suggests that Classics' marketing strategy remained less proactive than might be assumed.

What makes *Arthurian Romances* additionally important in the context of Penguin's medieval French titles of the 1980s and 1990s is the wealth of evidence it provides as to intended and actual audiences, since its file is rather more complete than those for other contemporaneous titles. We learn that Burgess, for example, was not the only academic party to have felt the lack of affordable translations of Chrétien's works. For instance, on 7 August 1990, a German doctoral student named Martin Milius enquires as to whether Penguin will ever produce a translation of Chrétien's works as well as of various other Arthurian tales.[35] Furthermore, Kibler provides Sarah Smith in Publicity (30 January 1991) with an extensive list of potential readers from amongst his and Carroll's contacts in both Europe and the United States, including individuals, journals and societies – all of which are academic. Carroll, under separate cover, additionally provides Keegan with further suggestions of academic review outlets (30 September 1991). What is clear, then, is that it took the particularly stoic commitment of academics to see Chrétien's works published in the Classics list, most specifically Burgess's cajoling of Keegan and Kibler. In all cases, the push was made with academic audiences in mind.

Kibler, as we saw, was initially a reluctant Penguin translator, but even he submitted a proposal for yet another medieval French title shortly before *Arthurian Romances* was published. In a letter to Keegan (19 October 1989), Kibler makes a cogent and impassioned case for an edition of Wace's *Roman de Brut*, something he says that he and Burgess agree upon as a desideratum:

---

[35] Particularly interesting are Keegan's notes to himself written on this letter, and the subsequent response he sends to Milius (23 August 1990), in which he confuses the Vulgate *Lancelot* about which Milius enquires with Chrétien's *Lancelot*, and also seems also not to realise that *The Quest of the Holy Grail* has already been published by Classics, which suggests he may not have been entirely knowledgeable about his medieval French titles.

Wace's *Brut*, aside from being the source for Layamon's work of the same name, is an exceptionally important Arthurian text in its own right – the first to introduce the Celtic matter into French. . . . The entire nature of the work changes from pseudo-history to romance, and it is written in a particularly lively and descriptive style. I know that with the ever increasing interest in things Arthurian, this text will sell exceptionally well.

Interestingly, then, Kibler does not explicitly promote the academic market in making his case but rather seems to cite a more general growing interest in Arthuriana. This should, we would think, speak straight to Penguin's preferred mode of operating, but strangely the project never seems to have been taken up. Kibler, in an email to me on 20 November 2018, said that he does not recall ever receiving a response, so he cannot be sure why the idea was not taken forward. Did Kibler perhaps miss a trick in not referring to the academy – maybe having been duped into doing so by the outward-facing positioning of Classics as for the general reader? Was Penguin, by now, more prepared to embrace the academic market openly?

4 Conclusion

In reaching the end of this study of medieval French titles as Penguin Classics, and specifically my consideration of how Penguin walked the tightrope between the general reader and the academic, I am struck by how consistently supportive of the hypotheses I presented in Section 2 were the archival findings set out in Section 3. Each and every title's editorial file tells a story that indicates that Penguin's outward-facing strategy for medieval French Classics, particularly in the United Kingdom, was to promote fervently the general reader angle whilst, behind the scenes, academics (often, though not always, external to Penguin) quietly manoeuvred the operation with a different agenda in mind.[36] Furthermore, we

[36] The notion of each file telling a story is one I borrow from Hare (1995, p. xv). He states: 'each file in the archive – when it has not been rendered meaningless by the

have seen that this practice barely changed across the course of around forty years, even in spite of fairly obvious developments in the marketplace and broader environment, in particular the expansion of higher education in both the United States and the United Kingdom but also the rise of intellectual culture, access to primary and secondary education, changing class relations and communications and information technology advancements in post-war Britain more generally. This is not to say, of course, that Penguin's seemingly haphazard approach was unsuccessful – on the contrary, medieval French titles enjoyed remarkable success, especially given their contents' relative obscurity in an anglophone context. However, the evidence from the Archive demonstrates that Penguin remained reluctant to accept or acknowledge openly the UK university market, even in spite of the large numbers of sales driven by it. Even by the time that Chrétien's works eventually made it to press, commercial success with medieval French titles seems largely to have come about because of external 'urgings' from academics.

Baldick and, especially, Radice, who had taken over the running of Penguin Classics in the 1960s, should however be credited for recognising the external shift and slowly and quietly introducing features to Classics that would enable their more effective use, though crucially not their explicit promotion, amongst academic readers. Radice (1984, p. 17) herself would state: 'Classical teaching was changing and I saw that there was a great opportunity for the classics to meet new demands if new titles were provided with line references, notes, indexes, bibliographies and fuller introductions, designed for use in teaching courses.' The challenge, however, was striking a balance between Classics' original conception under Rieu and their actual use, so as not to diminish the illusion of the general reader as the core audience. Radice's son William Radice (1987, p. 22) would describe it as demanding

> to produce books that were authoritative works of scholar-
> ship and of high literary merit, as well as readable and

ravages of time, countless moves from office to office, ill-advised clear-outs and all the other tiny incidents over the years – has a story of its own.' My experience has certainly borne this out.

appealing in the manner of the early Penguin Classics. They
made Betty Radice's task far more strenuous than Rieu's,
and far more open to attack, from scholars and academics on
the one hand, from poets and aesthetes on the other. The
sheer strenuousness of her task, and the difficulty of pleasing
such diverse and specialized groups (not the 'general reader'
of the Rieu years), was the first reason why the sunshine of
her years of collaboration with Rieu faded, making the
experience far cloudier and stormier than he had known.

Indeed, the evidence from the editorial files supports William Radice's
assertion that ideas about the Classics series' mission were firmly
entrenched at Penguin, and that much conflict, both internal and external,
would arise as Radice attempted 'tactical revision', as she (quoted in Hare,
1995, p. 188) would later term her careful treading of the line between the
educational and general reader markets. Williams (quoted in Hare, 1995,
p. 301) also corroborates this state of affairs, noting that '[o]verseeing
a major change in policy could not be undertaken without hurting feelings',
and it is perhaps for this reason that some confusion about what it was that
a Penguin Classic was supposed to do – in terms of marketing, editorial/
stylistic policy and communications – remained for years to come, even as
late as the 1980s when *Arthurian Romances* would eventually be put into
production.

In the end, then, on Penguin's side at least, success in publishing
medieval French literature seems to have been more a product of intuition
and fortunate timing than of hard-nosed tactics, much as we witnessed was
true of Allen Lane's wider endeavours under the Penguin umbrella. As
Morpurgo (1979, p. 219) observes: '[u]ninformed, but prescient
decisions . . . – and there are many in the history of Penguin – confirm
the view of Allen as a leader whose gifts were largely instinctive.' Lane was
not strategic in the traditional sense, in other words, but this did not prevent
him coming to be known as 'the greatest educative communicator of all
time', as Jonathan Cape described him in 1975 (quoted in Penguin Books,
1985, p. 83). So perhaps the success of these medieval French Penguin
Classics titles is due to one of the other consistencies noted in this Element:

the consideration of unsolicited proposals. Penguin appears always to have listened to those who contacted it and been savvy in grasping opportunities as they presented themselves, as explained in its Silver Jubilee publication: 'every suggestion that reaches us from them is carefully weighed, and none is passed over without what seems to be good and sufficient reason' (Penguin Books, 1960, p. 36). Penguin's real secret to success with medieval French, then, may have been less in understanding the market, and more in placing its trust in the readers who made contact with it, who happened often to be academics. Whilst Boll (2016) concludes similarly in respect of Penguin Spanish and Latin American translations, it is important to acknowledge that different scenarios may be true in respect of Classics translations from other languages. The improving sociocultural conditions of post-war Britain notwithstanding, language learning was still not open to all (Daniels, 2018). We might thus reasonably assume that there would have been more in-house expertise available in some subjects (such as English and the classical languages) than in the modern and medieval languages of Europe. It is therefore entirely possible that Penguin was simply more informed in respect of its strategic selection of both texts and translators in those cases, as Rayner (2018) has shown in respect of the Classics edition of Malory's *Morte Darthur*.

In the process of researching this Element, whilst in the Weston Library's Open Shelves in Oxford, I was struck by the physical placement on the shelves of books about Penguin immediately alongside those dedicated to the history of the university presses of Oxford and Cambridge. In some respects, this illustrates particularly vividly, if only anecdotally, the pervasive, yet almost unconscious categorisation of Penguin's Books as academic by a wider public, just as we witnessed in a more official form in the Academic Book of the Future Project's 2015 poll. What I have demonstrated in this Element, using medieval French Classics as my lens, is more concretely why and how this is so. Despite Penguin's best efforts to furnish the general reader with a library of quality, affordable literature, in the end it was largely not the general reader that medieval French Classics reached. Penguin's endeavours, quite accidentally, coincided with an increase in student numbers in both the United Kingdom and the United States, the post-war rise in intellectual culture and the gradual democratisation of knowledge, as well as the many looming technological revolutions, which together created a market at just the right moment: since Penguin's Classics range had all the appearance of a canon, they spoke automatically to the higher-education market. The books were practically perfect for the new academic readers who needed to acquire affordable and suitable 'canonical' works, and Radice's judicious regime of furtive development only accentuated their suitability in that context. External forces in the shape of academics looking to meet the needs of their students thus inevitably took over. Therefore, given the impetus and agency of the academy in the publication of Penguin's medieval French Classics depicted in the archival finds explored in this Element, we should not be surprised at the perception of these Classics, and perhaps indeed the Classics list more generally, as primarily academic.

Bibliography

Primary Texts and Penguin Archive Files

Béroul (1978). *The Romance of Tristan*. Trans. A. Fedrick. Harmondsworth: Penguin. Archive file: DM1107/L230.

Burgess, G. S., trans. (1990). *The Song of Roland*. Harmondsworth: Penguin. Archive file: should appear in DM1952/Box 335: 532 (but no such file contained within; assumed lost).

Cable, J., trans. (1972). *The Death of King Arthur*. Harmondsworth: Penguin. Archive file: DM1952/Box 328: L255.

Chrétien de Troyes, (1990, rev. 2004). *Arthurian Romances*. Trans. W. W. Kibler and C. W. Carroll. Harmondsworth: Penguin. Archive file: DM1952/Box 335: 521.

Christine de Pizan, (2000). *The Book of the City of Ladies*. Trans. R. Brown-Grant. Harmondsworth: Penguin. Title too late for Archive.

Christine de Pizan, (1985). *The Treasure of the City of Ladies*. Trans. S. Lawson. Harmondsworth: Penguin. Archive file: DM1952/334: 453.

Froissart, J. (1968, repr. 1978). *Chronicles*. Trans. G. Brereton. Harmondsworth: Penguin. Archive file: DM1107/L200.

Marie de France, (1999). *The Lais of Marie de France*. Trans. G. S. Burgess and K. Busby. Harmondsworth: Penguin. Archive file: DM1952/Box 334: 476.

Matarasso, P. M. trans. (1971). *Aucassin and Nicolette and Other Tales*. Harmondsworth: Penguin. Archive file: DM1952/Box 328: 254.

Matarasso, P. M., trans. (1969). *The Quest of the Holy Grail*. Harmondsworth: Penguin. Archive file: DM1107/L220.

Sayers, D. L., trans. (1960, repr. 1965). *The Song of Roland*. Harmondsworth: Penguin. Archive file: DM1107/L75.

Secondary Sources

Baines, P. (2005). *Penguin by Design: A Cover Story 1935–2005*. London: Allen Lane.

De Bellaigue, E. (2001a). The Extraordinary Flight of Book Publishing's Wingless Bird. *Logos*, 12(2), 70–77.

De Bellaigue, E. (2001b). The Extraordinary Flight of Book Publishing's Wingless Bird – Part II. *Logos*, 12(3), 129–37.

De Bellaigue, E. (2001c). The Extraordinary Flight of Book Publishing's Wingless Bird – Part III. *Logos*, 12(4), 215–23.

Beveridge, W. (1942). *Social Insurance and Allied Services*. London: HMSO.

Bloch, M. (1961). *Feudal Society*. Chicago: University of Chicago Press.

Bloom, H. (1994). *The Western Canon: The Books and School of the Ages*. San Diego: Harcourt, Brace & Co.

Boll, T. (2016). Penguin Books and the Translation of Spanish and Latin American Poetry, 1956–1979. *Translation and Literature*, 25, 28–57.

Bradbury, M. (1985). Foreword. *Fifty Penguin Years: Published on the Occasion of Penguin Books' Fiftieth Anniversary*. Harmondsworth: Penguin, pp. 7–9.

Buckley, P., ed. (2010). *Penguin 75: Designers – Authors – Commentary (the Good, the Bad . . .)*. London: Penguin.

Cannadine, D. (2013). Growing Up With Penguin Books. In W. Wootten and G. Donaldson, eds., *Reading Penguin: A Critical Anthology*. Newcastle-upon-Tyne: Cambridge Scholars, pp. 91–109.

Carne-Ross, D. S. (1968). Penguin Classics: A Report on Two Decades. *Arion: A Journal of the Humanities and the Classics*, 7(3), 395–99.

Coetzee, J. M. (1993). What Is a Classic? *Current Writing: Text and Reception in Southern Africa*, 5(2), 7–24.

Collini, S. (2012). 'The Chatto List': Publishing Literary Criticism in Mid-Twentieth-Century Britain. *Review of English Studies*, 63(261), 634–63.

Collini, S. (2008). *Common Reading: Critics, Historians, Publics*. Oxford: Oxford University Press.

Crowe, R. (2012). How to Fillet a Penguin. In S. Harrison and C. Stray, eds., *Expurgating the Classics: Editing Out in Latin and Greek*. London: Bristol Classical Press, pp. 197–211.

Daniels, J. (2018). Pioneering, Consolidating and Monitoring: The Development of French Language Learning in England, 1960s–2000s, from the Perspective of a Middle-School Teacher. In N. McLelland and R. Smith, eds., *The History of Language Learning and Teaching*, 3 vols. Cambridge: Legenda, II, pp. 293–306.

Donaldson, G. (2013). Penguin English Library: A Really Good Start for the General Reader. In W. Wootten and G. Donaldson, eds., *Reading Penguin: A Critical Anthology*. Newcastle-upon-Tyne: Cambridge Scholars, pp. 118–23.

Edwards, R. (2008). Afterword. In R. Edwards, S. Hare and J. Robinson, eds., *Penguin Classics*. Exeter: Short Run Press for Penguin Collectors' Society, p. 141.

Eliot, H. (2018). *The Penguin Classics Book*. London: Particular Books.

Eliot, S. (2013). A Pre-history for Penguin. In W. Wootten and G. Donaldson, eds., *Reading Penguin: A Critical Anthology*. Newcastle-upon-Tyne: Cambridge Scholars, pp. 1–26.

Eliot, T. S. (1945). What is a Classic? London: Faber; reprinted in Eliot, T. S. (1957). *Of Poetry and Poets*. New York: Farrar, Straus and Cudahy, pp. 53–71.

Fernández-Armesto, F. (2018). Firing the Canon. *The Times Higher Education Supplement*, 16 Aug. www.timeshighereducation.com/opinion/firing-canon

Getty, M. (1955). The Penguin Classics. *The Phoenix*, 9(3), 127–29.

Gorak, J. (1991). *The Making of the Modern Canon: Genesis and Crisis of a Literary Idea*. Atlantic Heights, NJ & London: Athlone.

Grant, M. (1960). The Teacher. In *Penguins Progress 1935–1960: Published on the Occasion of the Silver Jubilee of Penguin Books*. Harmondsworth: Penguin, pp. 19–21.

Grant, M. (2016). Historizing Citizenship in Post-War Britain. *The Historical Journal*, 59(4), 1187–206.

Guillory, J. (1995). *Cultural Capital: The Problem of Literary Canon Formation*. Chicago: University of Chicago Press.

Hare, S. (2015). *Penguin Scribe: A Collection of Articles on Penguin Books by Steve Hare*. London: Penguin Collectors' Society.

Hare, S. (2008a). A History of Penguin Classics. In R. Edwards, S. Hare and J. Robinson, eds., *Penguin Classics*. Exeter: Short Run Press for Penguin Collectors' Society, pp. 24–32.

Hare, S. (2008b). A Little Too English. In R. Edwards, S. Hare and J. Robinson, eds., *Penguin Classics*. Exeter: Short Run Press for Penguin Collectors' Society, pp. 54–57.

Hare, S. (2006). Reading the Classics. *Creative Review*, 25(11), 54–58.

Hare, S., ed. (1995). *Penguin Portrait: Allen Lane and the Penguin Editors 1935–1970*. London: Penguin.

Harris, J. (1997). *William Beveridge: A Biography*. Oxford: Clarendon.

Hilliard, C. (2006). *To Exercise Our Talents: The Democratization of Writing in Britain*. Cambridge, MA: Harvard University Press.

Hoggart, R. (1960). The Reader. In *Penguins Progress 1935–1960: Published on the Occasion of the Silver Jubilee of Penguin Books*. Harmondsworth: Penguin, pp. 27–29.

Hornsey, R. (2018). 'The Penguins Are Coming': Brand Mascots and Utopian Mass Consumption in Interwar Britain. *Journal of British Studies*, 57, 812–39.

Howard, M. S. (1971). *Jonathan Cape: Publisher*. London: Jonathan Cape.

Humble, N. (2011). Sitting Forward of Sitting Back: Highbrow v. Middlebrow Reading. *Modernist Cultures*, 6(1), 41–59.

Huxford, G. (2018). *The Korean War in Britain: Citizenship, Selfhood and Forgetting*. Manchester: Manchester University Press.

Joliffe, J. (1968). Medieval Gossip. *The Times Literary Supplement*, 3460, 649.

Jones, A. (2016). There is no such thing as 'the general reader'. OK? *Alison Jones Blog*, 22 November. https://alisonjones.com/there-is-no-such-thing-as-the-general-reader-ok.

Kermode, F. (1976). A Modern Way with the Classic. *New Literary History*, 5(3), 415–34.

Kermode, F. (1975). *The Classic: Literary Images of Permanence and Change*. New York: Viking; London: Faber & Faber.

Kolbas, E. D. (2001). *Critical Theory and the Literary Canon*. New York: Perseus.

Laity, P. (2014). Pelican Books take flight again. *The Guardian*, 25 April. www.theguardian.com/books/2014/apr/25/pelican-books-take-flight-relaunch

Lamb, L. (1952). Penguin Books: Style & Mass Production. *The Penrose Annual*, 46, 39–42.

Lane, A. (1938a). Books for the Million . . .. *Left Review*, 3(16), 968–70.

Lane, A. (1938b). Penguins and Pelicans. *The Penrose Annual*, 40, 40–42; reprinted in Moran, J. ed., (1974). *Printing in the 20th Century: A Penrose Anthology*. London: Northwood, pp. 159–62.

Lane, A. (1935). All About the Penguin Books. *The Bookseller*, 22, 497.

Lewis, J. (2006). *Penguin Special: The Life and Times of Allen Lane*. London: Penguin.

Lyons, W. J. (2013). Dead Sea Scrolls and Penguins: A Relationship in Fragments. In W. Wootten and G. Donaldson, eds., *Reading Penguin: A Critical Anthology*. Newcastle-upon-Tyne: Cambridge Scholars, pp. 65–90.

Macaluso, M. and Macaluso, K. (2018). *Teaching the Canon in 21st Century Classrooms: Challenging Genres*. Leiden: Brill.

McAteer, C. L. (2017). A Study of Penguin's Russian Classics (1950–1964) with Special Reference to David Magarshack. PhD thesis, University of Bristol.

McCleery, A. (2002). The Return of the Publisher to Book History: The Case of Allen Lane. *Book History*, 5, 161–85.

Morpurgo, J. E. (1979). *Allen Lane: King Penguin – A Biography*. London: Hutchinson & Co.

Orwell, G. (1936). Review of Penguin Books. *New English Weekly*, 5 March; reprinted in Orwell, S. and Angus, I., eds. (1968). *The Collected Essays, Journalism and Letters of George Orwell*, 4 vols. London: Secker & Warburg, I, pp. 165–67.

Papadima, L., Damrosch, D. and d'Haen, T. (2011). *The Canonical Debate Today: Crossing Disciplinary and Cultural Boundaries*. Amsterdam and New York: Rodopi.

Penguin Books (1985). *Fifty Penguin Years: Published on the Occasion of Penguin Books' Fiftieth Anniversary*. Harmondsworth: Penguin.

Penguin Books (1960). *Penguins Progress 1935–1960: Published on the Occasion of the Silver Jubilee of Penguin Books*. Harmondsworth: Penguin.

Pratt, B. (2008a). Founding Father: E. V. Rieu. In R. Edwards, S. Hare and J. Robinson, eds., *Penguin Classics*. Exeter: Short Run Press for Penguin Collectors' Society, pp. 8–15.

Pratt, B. (2008b), Nursing Mother: Betty Radice. In R. Edwards, S. Hare and J. Robinson, eds., *Penguin Classics*. Exeter: Short Run Press for Penguin Collectors' Society, pp. 16–23.

Radice, B. (1984). A Classic Education. *The Times Higher Education Supplement*, 19 October, 17.

Radice, B. (1969). The Penguin Classics: A Reply. *Arion: A Journal of the Humanities and the Classics*, 8(1), 130–8.

Radice, W. (2008). Introduction. In R. Edwards, S. Hare and J. Robinson, eds., *Penguin Classics*. Exeter: Short Run Press for Penguin Collectors' Society, pp. 5–7.

Radice, W. (1987). Introduction. In W. Radice and B. Reynolds, *The Translator's Art: Essays in Honour of Betty Radice*. Harmondsworth: Penguin, pp. 9–30.

Raven, J. (2014). The Industrial Revolution of the Book. In L. Howsam, ed., *The Cambridge Companion to the History of the Book*. Cambridge: Cambridge University Press, pp. 143–61.

Rayner, S. J. (2018). Penguin and the Shipwrecked Malory Project. *Poetica*, 88, 97–105.

Rieu, E. V. (1946). The Penguin Classics. *Penguins Progress*. 1, 48.

Roche, M. W. (2004). The Literary Canon and the Literary Critic in the Twenty-First Century. In M. W. Roche, *Why Literature Matters in the Twenty-First Century*. New Haven, CT and London: Yale University Press, pp. 249–60.

Rose, J. (2001). *The Intellectual Life of the British Working Classes*. New Haven and London: Yale University Press.

Rylance, R. (2005). Reading with a Mission: The Public Sphere of Penguin Books. *Critical Quarterly*, 47(3), 48–66.

Sanders, A. (2013). Hatching Classics. In W. Wootten and G. Donaldson, eds., *Reading Penguin: A Critical Anthology*. Newcastle-upon-Tyne: Cambridge Scholars, pp. 111–16.

Schmoller, T. (2008). Roundel Trouble. In R. Edwards, S. Hare and J. Robinson, eds., *Penguin Classics*. Exeter: Short Run Press for Penguin Collectors' Society, pp. 58–68.

Schorley, D. and McCann, W. (1985). *Fifty Years of Penguins: Catalogue of an Exhibition at Stranmillis College and the Universtiy [sic] of Ulster at Belfast, October to December 1985*. Belfast: Stranmillis College.

Sharp, J. P. (2000). *Condensing the Cold War: Readers' Digest and American Identity*. Minneapolis: University of Minnesota Press.

Simon, B. (1991). *Education and the Social Order: 1940–1990*. London: Lawrence & Wishart.

Smith, H. (2010). Book fan reveals collection of 15,000 Penguin paperbacks. *Metro*, 31 August. https://metro.co.uk/2010/08/31/book-fan-reveals-collection-of-15000-penguin-paperbacks-3436449/

Squires, C. (2007). *Marketing Literature: The Making of Contemporary Writing in Britain.* Basingstoke: Palgrave.

Steedman, C. (1986). *Landscape for a Good Woman.* London: Virago.

Todd, S. (2014). *The People: The Rise and Fall of the Working Class, 1910–2010.* London: John Murray.

Vale, M. (1968). Medieval Gossip. *The Times Literary Supplement*, 3455, 16 May, p. 508.

Walkerdine, V. (1997). *Daddy's Girl: Young Girls and Popular Culture.* Cambridge, MA: Harvard University Press.

Waples, D. (1931). What Subjects Appeal to the General Reader? *The Library Quarterly: Information, Community, Policy*, 1(2), 189–203.

Whiteside, N. (2014). The Beveridge Report and Its Implementation: A Revolutionary Project? *Histoire@Politique*, 3(24), 24–37.

Williams, W. E. (1956). *The Penguin Story MCMXXXV–MCMLVI.* Harmondsworth: Penguin.

Wood, S. (1985). *'A Sort of Dignified Flippancy': Penguin Books 1935–1960, to Accompany the Collection in Edinburgh University Library.* Edinburgh: Edinburgh University Press.

Wootten, W. and Donaldson, G. (2013). Preface. In W. Wootten and G. Donaldson, eds., *Reading Penguin: A Critical Anthology.* Newcastle-upon-Tyne: Cambridge Scholars, pp. xi–xv.

Yates, M. (2008). What Is a Penguin Classic? In R. Edwards, S. Hare and J. Robinson, eds., *Penguin Classics.* Exeter: Short Run Press for Penguin Collectors' Society, pp. 33–7.

Yates, M. (2006). *The Penguin Companion.* London: Penguin Collectors' Society.

Acknowledgements

In completing this Element, there are various people and organisations to whom I would like to express my sincerest thanks for their help and support.

I must start with Dr Samantha (Sam) Rayner and Dr Rebecca (Bex) Lyons, with whom I conceived the broader scope of our 'Medieval Penguin' project. Between them, they have given me endless hints and tips for useful sources of information and possible directions in which to take my study. Sam read my final manuscript and spotted areas to develop that my by then glazed eyes had missed, while Bex worked tirelessly as a research intern for me, thanks to funding from the University of Bristol's Faculty of Arts Research Intern scheme. As part of this, Bex created a digital repository of images in the summer of 2017 that meant I could hit the ground running during my year of research leave in 2018/19, which was generously granted by the University of Bristol.

I have benefitted enormously from the cheerful patience of Hannah Lowery and Michael Richardson in the University of Bristol's Special Collections, where the Penguin Archive is housed. They helped me to find files and even allowed me to send 'subs' to check references and the like whilst I was away. They also put me in touch with Joanna Prior at Penguin, who granted permission for the project team to use the Archive. Sarah McMahon and Jo Byrne at Penguin Random House subsequently agreed to extend those permissions, and Rachael Harrison in the Permissions team agreed to the citation of previously unpublished material.

Several organisations have sponsored my research on this topic, either through grants or access to materials, and without them, I could not have completed it. The Stationers' Foundation, through a Francis Mathew Travel Bursary, enabled me to travel to New York to access materials on the Penguin US operation, and Fordham University (particularly thanks to the sponsorship of Dr Nicholas Paul) granted me Visiting Fellow status whilst there so as to have unfettered access to library resources. Thanks to Dr Steve Rayner's sponsorship, Somerville College, Oxford (Dorothy Sayers's former college) gave me Academic Visitor status, meaning I could access the Bodleian's wealth of secondary materials every day for a month. During that stay, Steve and other generous friends provided accommodation. These included Dr Richard Allen and Mikal Mast and Dr Helen Swift, who organised an SCR room at St Hilda's College, Betty Radice's alma mater, no less! Durham University granted me a Holland Fellowship during which I was able to put the finishing touches to my manuscript. I am also grateful to my fellow scholars attending the international congresses on medieval studies in Leeds and Kalamazoo, as well as those at International Arthurian Society meetings, for listening to my ideas and remembering what they knew about the appearance of Penguins from the 1960s onwards. I must thank Professor Jane Taylor in particular, for she put me in touch with Pauline Matarasso who, in turn, allowed me to interview her, as did Professor Glyn Burgess and Professor Keith Busby. Their personal recollections of their relationships with Penguin were a gold mine of useful (and often amusing) information. Dr Grace Huxford also made excellent suggestions for how to contextualise my study within the wider landscape of the post-war period.

Finally, I would like to thank my friends and family for their unceasing support. In this and in all endeavours, they are always there and for that I am incredibly grateful. Chief amongst them is my husband, Dr Benjamin Pohl, who showed unusual enthusiasm for my project, even though the only manuscripts to be seen in it were, for his taste, about 800–900 years too new. As with all my work, Ben read it and critiqued it with remarkable patience. He even served as one of my 'subs' in the Penguin Archive. This book is thus dedicated both to him and to my best friend and big-sis-2, Sam, the true driving force behind 'Medieval Penguin'.

Permission to cite Dorothy Sayers's correspondence: © The Trustees of Anthony Fleming (deceased) by Permission of David Higham Associates.

Permission to cite previously unpublished material from the Penguin Archive: © Penguin Books Ltd. The author would especially like to thank Pauline Matarasso, Glyn Burgess, Peter Ghosh, Karen Braziller, William Kibler and Keith Busby for both checking the sections of this Element that cite their correspondence with Penguin and agreeing to their publication.

Funding Information

This book was kindly supported by the Stationers' Foundation.

THE

STATIONERS'
FOUNDATION

Cambridge Elements

Publishing and Book Culture

Series Editor
Samantha Rayner
University College London

Samantha Rayner is Reader in UCL's Department of Information Studies. She is also Director of UCL's Centre for Publishing, co-director of the BloomsburyCHAPTER (Communication History, Authorship, Publishing, Textual Editing and Reading) and co-editor of the Academic Book of the Future BOOC (Book as Open Online Content) with UCL Press.

Associate Editor
Rebecca Lyons
University of Bristol

Rebecca Lyons is Teaching Fellow at the University of Bristol. She is also co-editor of the experimental BOOC (Book as Open Online Content) at UCL Press. She teaches and researches book and reading history, particularly female owners and readers of Arthurian literature in fifteenth- and sixteenth-century England, and also has research interests in digital academic publishing.

Advisory Board:

About the Series:

This series aims to fill the demand for easily accessible, quality texts available for teaching and research in the diverse and dynamic fields of Publishing and Book Culture. Rigorously researched and peer-reviewed Elements will be published under themes, or 'Gatherings'. These Elements should be the first check point for researchers or students working on that area of publishing and book trade history and practice: we hope that, situated so logically at Cambridge University Press, where academic publishing in the UK began, it will develop to create an unrivalled space where these histories and practices can be investigated and preserved.

Cambridge Elements

Publishing and Book Culture
Academic Publishing

Gathering Editor: Jane Winters

Jane Winters is Professor of Digital Humanities at the School of Advanced Study, University of London. She is co-convenor of the Royal Historical Society's open-access monographs series, New Historical Perspectives, and a member of the International Editorial Board of Internet Histories and the Academic Advisory Board of the Open Library of Humanities.

ELEMENTS IN THE GATHERING

The General Reader and the Academy: Medieval French Literature and Penguin Classics
Leah Tether

Printed in the United States
By Bookmasters